Theater Artists Making Theatre With No Theater

▼

Spring 2020

A Collection of Works Compiled by
Sheila Callaghan, Kelly Miller, and Meg Miroshnik

AN IMPRINT OF
SAVAGE CANDY PRODUCTIONS, INC.

Copyright © 2020.
All Rights Reserved.

All the material within *Theater Artists Making Theatre With No Theater* is fully protected under the copyright laws of the United States of America, the British Commonwealth, including Canada, and all other countries of the Copyright Union. All rights, including professional and amateur stage productions, recitation, lecturing, public reading, motion picture, radio broadcasting, television and the rights of translation into foreign languages are strictly reserved.

Print edition.
ISBN: 978-1-7341402-2-4

tripwireharlot.com.

-CONTRIBUTORS-

Liz Duffy Adams • Nayna Agrawal • Tessa Albertson • Jazmine Aluma • Liz Appel • Mallery Avidon • Rachel Axler • Jenny Lyn Bader • Kari Bentley-Quinn • Kate Bergstrom • Susan Bernfield • Larry Biederman • Rachel Bonds • Amy Boratko • Mattie Brickman • Eleanor Burgess • Adrienne Campbell-Holt • Jonathan Caren • Marisa Carr • Jaime Castañeda • Jo Cattell • Jennifer Chambers • Jackie Chung • Carmela Corbett • Adam D. Crain • Cusi Cram • Migdalia Cruz • Francisca Da Silveira • Mashuq Deen • Steph Del Rosso • Kristoffer Diaz • Julie Felise Dubiner • Erik Ehn • Larissa FastHorse • Annch Feinberg • Liz Frankel • Gibson Frazier • Matt Freeman • Edith Freni • Jeremy Gable • Joanna Glum • Emma Goidel • Jacqueline Goldfinger • Isaac Gómez • Tasha Gordon-Solmon • Kirsten Greenidge • Rinne Groff • Jason Grote • Lauren M. Gunderson • April Dawn Guthrie • Mary Elizabeth Hamilton • Adrien-Alice Hansel • Elizabeth Harper • Julie Hébert • Justice Hehir • Laura Heisler • Alex Henrikson • Deb Hiett • Daniel Hirsch • Lily Holleman • Jess Honovich • Scott Horstein • Andy Horwitz • Emma Horwitz • Lily Houghton • Lindsay Brandon Hunter • Kristin Idaszak • Naomi Iizuka • Rachel Jendrzejewski • Kate Jopson • Lila Rose Kaplan • MJ Kaufman • Lucas Kavner • Lisa Kenner Grissom • Callie Kimball • Ramona Rose King • Krista Knight • Andrea Kuchlewska • Jenni Lamb • Jacqueline E. Lawton • Jer Adrianne Lelliott • Sarah Rose Leonard • Sofya Levitsky-Weitz • Danielle Levsky • Mike Lew • Jerry Lieblich • Katie Lindsay • Craig Lucas • Kirk Lynn • Wendy MacLeod • Jennifer Maisel • Chelsea Marcantel • Kelly Miller • Winter Miller • Rehana Lew Mirza • Michael Mitnick • Anne G. Morgan • Matt Moses • Allie Moss • Gregory S. Moss • Rebecca Mozo • Nick Hadikwa Mwaluko • Katie Locke O'Brien • Kira Obolensky • Laurel Ollstein • Matthew Paul Olmos • Julie Oullette • Kristen Palmer • Lina Patel • Christopher O. Peña • Roxie Perkins • Eric Pfeffinger • Rebecca Phillips Epstein • Daria Polatin • Christina Quintana (CQ) • Stella Fawn Ragsdale • Molly Rice • Anya Richkind • Colette Robert • Alexis Roblan • Ashley Lauren Rogers • Elaine Romero • Whitney Rowland • Zoe Sarnak • Matt Schatz • Dana Schwartz • Betty Shamieh • Mike Shapiro • Alexandra Shilling • Jen Silverman • Jessy Lauren Smith • Elizabeth Spreen • Matt Stadelmann • Ellen Steves • Caridad Svich • Adam Szymkowicz • Kate Tarker • Ashley Teague • Melisa Tien • Ken Urban • Kathryn Walat • John Walch • Molly Ward • Seanan Palmero Waugh • Tatiana Wechsler • Jenny Rachel Weiner • Calamity West • Deborah Yarchun • Mackenzie Yeager • Gina Young

-TABLE OF CONTENTS-

FOREWORD viii

I. THE EMAIL 1

II. THE INVITATION 5

III. THE ARTWORK 25

ACKNOWLEDGEMENTS 319

-FOREWORD-

Roughly two months after the novel coronavirus pandemic hit, three theater pals (Sheila Callaghan, Kelly Miller, and Meg Miroshnik) sent out a mass email to all the theater artists they knew and loved (and a bunch they loved but didn't know yet) asking for some artwork. They had no idea what would come back to them, but they knew they wanted to create something that felt like community.

Their bcc list included actors, dramaturgs, playwrights, directors, designers, AD's, composers, and literary managers from around the country and all corners of the field. Almost immediately, people began sending work. The response was fervent and breathtaking. And so…

This book! Which contains **every piece of art** collected in the weeks that followed. It functions as a snapshot of life in quarantine prior to the murder of George Floyd on May 25th, 2020. Also included is a reproduction of the initial email and a series of related internet links.

Note: the artwork is arranged in alphabetical order according to the artist's last name, and the caption for each piece can be found on the page ***following*** the artwork. This is intended to evoke a sense of theatricality; the piece itself sets a certain expectation for the viewer, which is then immediately re-contextualized by the simple turn of a page.

At its core, this capsule is a platform for fellowship and creativity amongst a handful of artists. **However.** It may also function as a foghorn blast through the gloom during a moment of unprecedented crisis in our industry as all our stages remain dark; a time of no audiences, no in-person live performance, no group gatherings, and no theater.

Simply put, these pages are a way of saying, **we are still here.**

— Sheila, Kelly, and Meg,
Oct. 20, 2020

I.

-THE EMAIL-

from:	Sheila Callaghan, Meg Miroshnik, & Kelly Miller
bcc:	(everyone)
date	May 3, 2020, 12:57 AM
subject:	our brai ns have go ne i nside out .

Hi, it's Sheila Callagha n, Kelly Miller, a nd Meg Mirosh nik. Meg wrote this email. Sheila a nd Kelly weighed i n o n it. Meg's keyboard is messed up right now a nd she watched a bu nch of Youtube tutorials a nd ca n't figure it out. Sheila a nd Kelly thought it was fu n ny.

We feel like our mi nds are i nside out. We've had a few lo ng pho ne co nversatio ns about this feeli ng. We're wo nderi ng a) if you're feeli ng that way too a nd b) what you are doi ng about it

If you're like " uhhhhhhhhhhhhhh" yeah us too.

⟵ PEOPLE CLICKED THAT

We have a n idea.

https://www.tripwireharlot.com/threetheatrepals
(do n't worry, that li nk goes to a site sheila hosted ☺.)

love,
us

II.

-THE INVITATION-

** [this is the page with the backstory]

Right before the world blew up, Meg and Kelly and Sheila were making something.

They'd met a couple years ago and formed The Kilroys with ten other gals, and now they were diving into a new project together: a multi-volume compilation of writings, musings, and interviews featuring the most amazing people on the planet. A container for the collective wisdom of others. A kind of artistic survival guide.

And then stuff went down and here we are.

We wondered if this project was possible anymore. Or useful. Or what advice even looks like right now. Or survival.

Our minds were turning inside out.

We asked each other a bunch of questions. Like: how do you create theatre with no theater?

And: what is the difference between content and comfort?

And: how do we get off our screens for like a millisecond?

And: how are we (YOU) documenting our (YOUR) real-time experience of this?

What if we're not?

Should we be?   *(cont.)*

| https://www.tripwireharlot.com/threetheatreoals

But...

...

How're we supposed to make things when we can't sit still for more than 20 minutes because anxiety disinfectant groceries masks wifi homeschooling illnesses economy alcohol parents income bodies kittens?

And then we were like...

...

...

...

...

...

We definitely wanna make stuff that feels like theatre without theater but we can't pretend to concentrate like it's January.

So what's the answer?

> > > > > > keep going   ← PEOPLE CLICKED THAT

click

** [this is the page with the idea]

No fucking clue.

But it actually doesn't matter.

...

...

Because...

Like…

Maybe you have something right about to fall out of your head.

Maybe it wants a witness.

Maybe you could drop it on an 8x5 template.

In black and white.

At 300 dpi.

Maybe you've already made it but don't know where to put it.

Maybe other people would want to see it.

Maybe it looks nothing like this: *(cont.)*

https://www.tripwireharlot.com/threetheatrepals

{ONE YEAR, One Day after the End.}

Dusk in a muddy, rat-infested country Inn-yard. NIM DULLYN *knocks on a door. His wrist bleeds.*

No response.

He knocks louder.

NIM

Oy!
Ope the *Door*.

Oy!
I got ear of him.

More knocking.

NIM

From Within:

MARGARET

Who's there?

NIM

A Friend.

The Door is opened a sliver.

MARGARET

What is a Friend?

NIM

Nim Dullyn who looks for the Player *Killingworth*.

The Door is shut up.

MARGARET

O, fuck off.
Our REVELS now are ended.
No *Players* no more.

NIM

But night last!
I heard *Killingworth* play Caliban in the Droll.

VOICE

Ho, that's a good laugh.

NIM

It WAS.
I *laughed*.
I laughed til I cried.
And my Year Long Curse of Silence of Grieff
was killed.

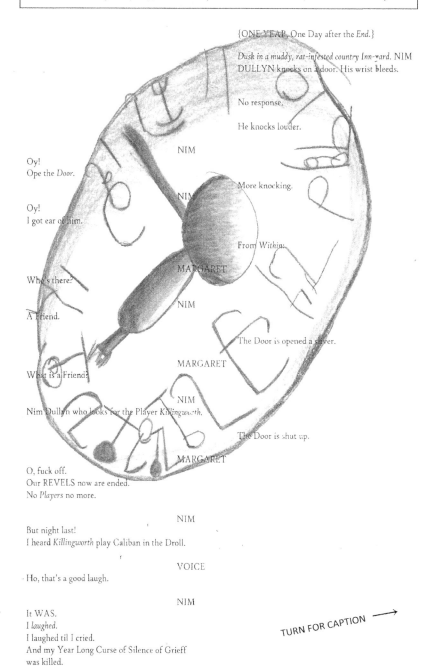

TURN FOR CAPTION →

"Time at Home," by Meg Miroshnik. A collaboration with Jacob Miroshnik on the occasion of his 4th birthday. April 13, 2020.

(cont.)

`https:// www.tripwireharlot.com/threetheatrepals`

Or this:

A love letter to my little brother, in the Time of Covid.

Sunday, April 12th, 2020

Today I found out my "little" brother, Matthew Edward Miller, is fighting for his life. Yesterday, his temperature was 103.4 and he's having trouble breathing. He's fighting alone, quarantined on the second floor of his own house. His wife Jena—a nurse—scrubbed the house until her fingers bled. She texts him from downstairs, nursing him as best she can from afar. They have two boys—Hayden (13) and Tyler (9)—blonde-haired, blue-eyed little Vikings like her, naturally athletic and charming like him. She is their fierce Protector, as he fights this alone upstairs.

My brother is 36, 6'3" and asthmatic—a terrifying combination right now. He's young, strong and he was healthy until this ravaged his body.

MY FAVORITE MEMORY OF HIM:

I still remember Matt as the kindest little boy with a bowl haircut and soft brown eyes. The first few years of elementary school, I would walk down to Old Providence to pick him up after school—and together, we would walk the long two blocks home. (I'm almost six years older than him and we were latchkey kids, spending afternoons watching TV, pretending to do our homework.)

One day after school, he was especially quiet. Then he started crying. Matt told me his friends had mocked another boy that day, that they'd been so cruel. And that against his better judgement, he'd joined them. He was beside himself. Upset. Ashamed. "No one deserves to be treated that way," he said. He cried all the way home, until we pulled out the white pages of our old telephone book to look up the boy's parents. He called them and asked for Mike, apologizing first to them and then to him.

That was the day I knew my brother would grow up to be the kindest of men. A protector of all.

MY BROTHER IS:
- Wise.
- Kind.
- Funny.
- Charming.
- Big-hearted.
- Gracious.
- Talented.
- An incredible musician.
- An incredible father.
- An incredible husband.
- An incredible host.
- An incredible athlete.
- The best gift giver I know.
- One of the best men I know.
- One of the best humans I know.
- My hero.

← *"A Love Letter To Matt Ed," by Kelly Miller.
A tribute to my little brother, the night I
found out I might lose him. April 12, 2020.*

(cont.)

`https://www.tripwireharlot.com/threetheatrepals`

Or this:

help.

"Moments After Confrontation with Blank Page on 53rd Day of Self-Isolation," by Sheila Callaghan. Conceived on the one year anniversary of her mother's death. May 7, 2020.

(cont.)

Maybe once you make it, you'll send it to us.

Maybe if we get 100 of them, we'll make a book called *Theater Artists Making Theatre With No Theater, Spring 2020*.

And maybe we'll publish it through Sheila's book company.

And then maybe you'll buy a copy to see what everyone else made.

Or you'll force your non-theater friends to buy it and say they got off easy since you didn't ask them to watch a staged reading of your Zoom play entitled *Quilting in Quarantine*.

And maybe the proceeds of the book will go to theater artists in need.

Which is pretty much all of them right now.

But maybe you don't really wanna make anything, actually.

...that's cool. We get it.

If that's the case...

You definitely don't wanna click **HERE**.   ← PEOPLE CLICKED THAT

click

| https:// www.tripwireharlot.com/threetheatrepals

** [this is the page with the instructions]

1) Start with a template (pick one):

    JPEG.   **PDF**.   **Word**.   **Pages**.

2) Make some theatre.

And by "theatre," we mean whatever comes to your mind when you consider making theatre right now in this format in this time in this headspace. Make it right on your computer, or print out a template and scan what you make, or take a well-lit high-definition pic of what you make (HDR instructions for iPhones here). You're welcome to make something that goes beyond the crop marks, but just know it might get cropped a little.

Your theatre can have rising action, climax, denouement, none of the above. It can have a villainous hero, a heroic villain, a vegetable, a planet, a neon tube. It can have the contents of one small part of your heart or one large part of your brain or a speck of dust on your eyelash. Whatever you like. Whatever you don't. As long as it's a <u>single page in black and white at 300 dpi</u>. (If you don't know from dpi, we googled it for you.)

3) Double-check you did it right. Have your theater friends double-check. Have them make one too.

4) Title it. Be aware the title will be shown after the piece, so the "reveal" may be considered part of the event. Here's the format we've been using: "Title Of Piece," by Author. Context for piece. Date created. *(cont.)*

5) Email it to megandsheilaandkelly@gmail.com. You'll get an automated response saying we got it.

If we get 100 correctly formatted pieces ONE WEEK FROM TODAY, *boom* we make a book. If we don't, *boom* we don't. Either way, we're so happy you did it. We're happy we did it too.

And just in case you're in a temporal fog right now, it's ***DATE.*** ***TIME***.

THESE UPDATED WHENEVER THE PAGE LOADED

Also, we miss you.

Love,
Sheila, Kelly, & Meg

boom

III.

-THE ARTWORK-

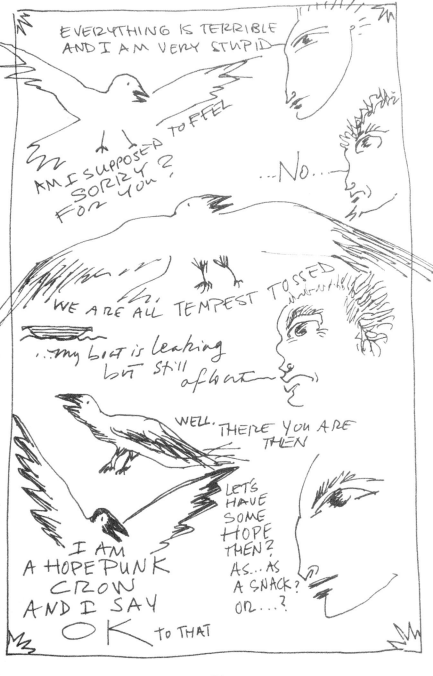

← *"Hopepunk Crow," by Liz Duffy Adams. On day sixty-five. May 15, 2020.*

WE'RE BESIDE THE GANGES RIVER (HOLY RIVER IN INDIA)

A fire. Not for s'mores. For somebody. A. BODY.

PANDIT

Om, jai, Jagdish, swahah.

Dressed in their finest, PAPA (48), MUMMY (39), and SIS (20) mourn, casting rice and holy water upon the crematory.

Then there's their daughter/sister: our widow, NEEMA (21). Her resting bitch face eclipses her contrite funeral attire: no makeup, no jewelry, no-frills sari.

MUMMY

Fix your face.

NEEMA

Will do. Once the crowd gets here.

SIS

You're so morbid.

NEEMA

Hope so. There's a corpse a burnin'

The fire crackles. The bones splinter. A thigh falls off.

PAPA

It's wrath!

NEEMA

It's physics. The femur is the heaviest bone in the human body.

MUMMY

He was the best son-in-law. Gifted us money, even before he married you.

NEEMA

He sharted, snored and didn't take his Lipitor unless I mixed it in his chai.

SIS

Cholesterol is a status symbol! All the upper castes have it.

MUMMY

Papa would kill for cholesterol!

Neema stares at her catatonic father.

← *"Honey Windows," by Nayna Agrawal. May 11th, 2020.*

START HERE!

I have some thoughts about my predicament and what it means for my 20's

23 in ISOLATION

4ever the Great Class of 2020

Things I'm worried I'll miss out on in my 20's while socially Distanced:

1) sex. when will I be touched again?
2) dating. when will I organically "meet" people again?
3) will my career suffer?
4) How will I process graduating?

The class that left our haven of friends in Middle March.

Things I'm living with in my 20s

1) I don't need to marry anyone soon so isolation is hot
2) Time to get crafty and focus on my deep core voice
3) Dogs are great investments
4) These are my 20s, so I'm not super interested in what yours were like.
5) Someone asked to be my sugar Daddy? Real job? I NEED JOB?
END OF PLAY.

I've grown up more in the last <9 weeks> Than most of senior year.

I have some thoughts: do I like what's become of me?
Can I consider myself a virgin by the time this is over?

← *"My 20's In Covid," by Tessa Albertson. May 18, 2020.*

Mother enters. She is tired, but strong; jaded, but hopeful; ragged, but beautiful. She is holding a laptop propped on her hip, like it could be a stack of schoolgirl books or a six-month-old baby. Her shoulders are bent inward, but her chin is up.

Mother: You see, we have done this before. We have walked into the unknown and watched everything we thought we understood about the world crumble into flakes of our former life, so transparent we can almost see, when we hold them to the light, an outline of who we once were.

Yes. We've done this before.

Do you remember the way you listened when they told you what it would be like? Like you already knew. But you didn't know. How could you? How could you even wrap your mind around it?

Do you remember what it was like when you realized that you had no idea? You had no fucking idea. Remember?

Mama 1 From the Audience: Yes, girl.

Mama 2 From the Audience: I remember.

Mother: You held this bundle, this baby, this bomb—eyes wide with shock. And you did it. You got through one day, and then another. And then another, until you were doing the thing. You were raising a child. Remember?

Remember how it hurt? How it hurt to do the small things like shit alone? Have a conversation? Feed yourself? Remember how it felt to reorganize your cells and your schedule, and make a new life—the one you never thought you'd be living?

And months later, do you remember what it was like to cry when all the tears were gone, because you had cried them all—rivers of the things you missed like brunches with your friends, and sleeping in, and dancing in a dark room full of sweaty bodies.

Remember what it was like not to worry, not to worry about a fucking thing?

Mama 1 From the Audience: Mmmm, hmmm.

Mother: You see, mamas of the world, we've done this before. We've walked into the nebulous optimisms, the long nights, the unknown. And we walked out with hard-earned joy, the kind no brunch can replace. We can do this. Because, you see, we've done this before.

"Nebulous Optimisms," by Jazmine Aluma. Upon completing the 67th day of quarantine, Monday, May 11th, 2020.

"a prayer for insomniacs," by Liz Appel. I've been having a really hard time sleeping and then this sunrise happened around 4:30 a.m. It reminded me to have faith in lost things. May 15, 2020.

honestly mostly my anxiety is better now

and I quit theatre already anyway. it's too heartbreaking.

I've been working at a bookstore. But now I don't do that either.

The bookstore is trying to make us go back to work and risk our lives for minimum wage because they got a PPP loan from the federal government that they have to use in eight weeks. And as of today Curbside pickup is ALLOWED for retail.

Do you have to do something just because you're allowed to?

I asked my manager why she was willing to risk her and her employees lives when it's clear that everyone should still just stay home.

I keep hoping that maybe the silver lining is capitalism will fail.

"an internal monologue," by Mallery Avidon. I live with my mother who turns 71 this month and I'm not going back to a minimum wage retail job. May 8, 2020.

ME, to myself, observing: My son wants to go outside.

ME, to myself, reflecting: I am afraid to take him outside.

(repeat forever)

← *"scared of air," by Rachel Axler. Mother's Day, 7:50am, but also every moment since March 11th or so, 2020.*

ACT I: What We Lost
- 1 blue notebook
- 2 theatre seasons
- 3-5 gigs
- more Americans than during the Vietnam War
- 2 drawings sketched by one of those lost Americans
- 1 5-lb. weight
- 17 hours of physical therapy
- 23 grandparent visits
- 1 college reunion
- 1 field day
- ½ a pajama
- our perception of time

ACT II: What We Learned
- Who will bake you a sourdough loaf and drop it off when you're having symptoms
- Why videoconference life causes headaches/soul aches
- How to fix and mount a broken curtain rod when you can't call the handyman
- How kids will try + even prefer non-dairy cheese slices when you can't find real cheese
- How to isolate from your family in your own home
- We've been washing our hands wrong our whole lives
- We took so much for granted for so long
- A watched pot does boil. Eventually.
  —A 15-year-old can prove it, too.

ACT III: What Next
- Transcending it all, we'll know how soon
- Becoming new, with less handshaking and more trees
- ?

"Pandemic Lists: *A Play in Three Acts," by Jenny Lyn Bader. Conceived during 33 days of indoor quarantine and written on May 15, 2020.*

This is a hard time for us right now

but for you, there is so much ahead in the next few years

You will be allowed to cross the street by yourself

You will have a best friend and she will move away
and you will feel heartbreak for the first time
You will get your first diary
You will write your first book of poems on a typewriter about whales

This is when you are becoming a writer

Your teachers will tell you that you talk too much. You will be told you are too much of everything. You will spend too much time making yourself smaller. You are going to hide your light under a bushel for a time longer than is fair.

In thirty years your own voice will still scare you
I wish I could show you how not to be scared.

"Monologue to Little Me at a Difficult Time," by Kari Bentley-Quinn. Created in a two martini tearful trip down memory lane in Queens (the epicenter of the pandemic). May 2020.

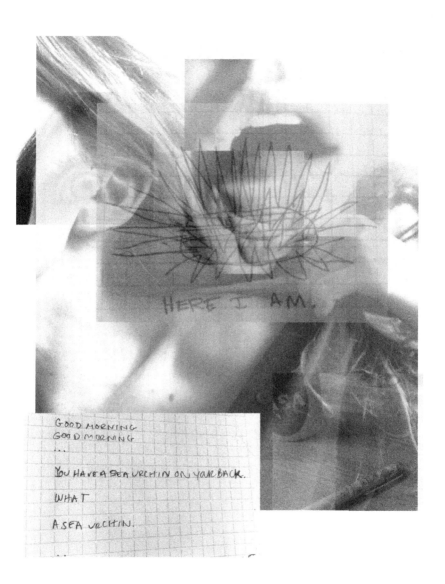

"In 2019 sea urchins devastated kelp forests off of California's coast. To combat the problem, humans started to eat the sea urchins more and more rapidly. It was too late. Many of these kelp forests are now barren. The only edible part of a sea urchin are its gonads. You eat these raw while the creature is still living. You bite the matter by the balls. It tastes good, but there is also the failure, there is also the fact that you had never supported the lives of the real experts in the first place," by Kate Bergstrom. In New York, a Californian two months into quarantine, unable to see my mother. May 11, 2020.

he won't talk about food
                              what do I want for dinner
              who cares what's for dinner   why are you
                        asking   why does
              everybody talk about food   all the
       time   planning food, what is that, what the
                there is nothing interesting about dinner
but
                    won't talk about it
but everybody
                                            won't
       but
but obvious reasons
hey
you're French / kinda French
you should know this
it's how you
your people / kinda / uncles aunts
sit for hours over
and that's just lunch
lookit not saying this well maybe
it's how you respond
it's how you make comfort
it's how you make event
people need something to look forward
okay I
something to / here we are HI!
sit together over to make a
a thing / a thing a thing that
every other person in this #@&* world okay
is talking about food enjoying food enjoying
comfort enjoying each / appreciating each other
demonstrating care turns out you are the only person
!!!in the world!!!
who won't and I have only got
you
the dinner it's like it's like it's like it's like a metaphor
IT'S NOT ABOUT THE DINNER

← *"nor does he drink," by Susan Bernfield. It's how last Saturday afternoon went, tomorrow is another Saturday. May 15, 2020.*

"Hyper-FOMO," or, "Face of Aspiring Theatre Director Reading Welcome, Clever, and Thoughtful Invitation to Create Theatre* (*and by 'theatre,' he means whatever came to his mind when he considered making theatre right now in this format in this time in this headspace) After Realizing It Took Him a Week to Read this Invitation and the Due Date is Now," by Larry Biederman. Minutes after submitting final semester grades and finally catching up on email. May 15, 2020.

←

I went to New York because I wanted to go somewhere where I could breathe, and be wildly alone.

Because I knew I needed to write something to get to the other side of my grief.

And New York   was a   place I   could write.

I needed to write something to get to the other side of my grief.
Or through the first wave.
I didn't know then that there would be countless waves.
Waves forever.

Swim through it! my dad would yell at me as we stood on the sandbar, the water up to our chests, a wave curling toward us, *Swim through it! If you turn and try to go back, that's when you get dashed on the ocean floor!*

And here we are now, on the ocean floor.
Walking through the hours, pushing against a sea of information, grief, fear. The pressure is immense. Enough to crush one's bones, certainly one's heart. But on we press, enduring, until we might swim to the surface, survey the wreckage, let the sun beat down on it all, on our faces, our aching chests. And we will breathe. And we will reach for each other.

"The Ocean Floor," by Rachel Bonds. Fragments of an essay I've been working on, and waves. May 14, 2020.

1.
Mama stands just outside the door and listens to the children play. A and B sit on a rug in the center of a ring of makeshift houses, and each holds tiny woodland animals, dressed in absurdly tiny calico clothing, in her hands.

A: C'mon Dashi, C'mon kids. Let's go. Do you want to go to the sleepover?

    B: I'm not old enough to go. I need to ask my mama.

A: Where is mama?

    B: I don't know.

A: She's missing!

    B: She's missing?

A: Let's find her.

    B: I bet she's hiding in the drawer.

Mama walks into the room, across the rug, and shrinks herself to the size of the mouse mama, the one who wears the brilliantly fuchsia satin dress. She tucks herself into the drawer filled with overalls. She is missing, for a moment. It is wonderful.

2.

A nibbles on a cookie. It is a sandwich cookie, half vanilla and half chocolate. It is most definitely a generic Oreo.

A: This makes me remember Maddie. And the Playscape. And Papa buying me Oreos from the café while sister swims. She stopped liking the Oreos, so Papa would buy her Pirate's Booty —which is made from the butts of pirates—and I would eat these cookies in the hallway and play.

A stands up, cookie crumbs falling onto her bare chest. She is there, in the chlorine-scented hallway outside the pool. It is normal, for a moment.

3.

In a tempest, B flails and weeps. We call this the storm of feelings, and it will pass.

B: I want to move to Antarctica. And be alone. And you can't come to my cozy, cozy cottage on the bottom of the earth. But please don't ever leave me, Mama.

B reaches out for Mama, holds her close. B closes her eyes for a moment and goes to the cozy, cozy cottage in Antarctica. A shiver runs through her body as she's warmed by Mama's arms.

"Mother's Day 59," by Amy Boratko. Using the real words of her daughters, Beatrice and Rosalind. May 10, 2020.

"Breakthrough," by Mattie Brickman. Upon arrival of Farm Cart. April 23, 2020.

*"Unprofessional," by Eleanor Burgess.
William wanted to be a Hydra. May 9, 2020.*

two hands touching

grass green
deep green
aquamarine

FOREVER

lemon
yellow
goldenrod
canary

Yves Klein
blue
royal blue
green blue
ocean depths

(no color here)

theater right now
feels like the translation of
these colors to black + white

"Adrienne & Esme," by Adrienne Campbell-Holt. I'm playing with watercolors for the first time in 10+ years and it feels so good. May 9, 2020.

decades of democratic decline. The answer is that the more astute and counterfeit democrats have figured out how to rig elections and get away with it. An increasing number of authoritarian leaders are contesting multiparty elections, but are unwilling to put their fate in the hands of voters; in other words, more elections are being held, but more elections are also being rigged.

This part of the story of global democratic backsliding and the inability of elections, on their own, to deliver democracy,⁷ has already received considerable academic attention and media coverage.⁸ Although international policymakers continue to demonstrate remarkable faith in the transformative power of elections, even those held in the most difficult of contexts, such as in Afghanistan and Iraq, recent experience has shown the enduring capacity of leaders to subvert multipartyism.⁹ What is less well known is that in many countries elections do not simply fail to topple dictators and despots, they sometimes actively help them shore up their grip on power. This is because reintroducing elections typically enables embattled governments to secure access to valuable political resources like foreign aid, while reinvigorating the ruling party and, in some cases, dividing the opposition. Consequently, a number of authoritarian regimes that appeared to be in their death throes have, with the help of the ballot box, managed not only to win consecutive elections, but also to establish their political dominance.¹⁰

To put it another way, authoritarian leaders can hold elections without losing their hold on power, take and repurpose their resources and legitimacy, while retaining their grip on power. This is not to say that autocrats welcome elections. Just as the reintroduction of multiparty politics to authoritarian party states, they do not see dissent and opposition as legitimate political activities. But once competitive elections have been reinstated, these regimes often prove to be remarkably adept at manipulating them for their own purposes. As a result, authoritarian systems that hold elections but do not allow opposition parties to meaningfully contest them prove to be more durable than those that do not.¹¹

This book is about why this is possible and how it happens. While a small number of authoritarian governments win elections through legitimate means, the majority adopt a range of strategies to ensure that they cannot lose. Thus, in many countries around the world the art of retaining power has become the art of electoral manipulation.

This is not to say that all elections are rigged, or that authoritarian leaders rely on rigging alone to win. In reality, savvy autocrats understand that it is far

"Reconstructed Creation Myth," by Jonathan Caren. Los Angeles. May 11, 2020.

ME
Jesus, why are my neighbors so loud?
Maybe I should call my ex.

ALSO ME
No, fuck that, he'll just be shitty and make you feel worse.

ME
Oh. Yeah, you're probably right. I mean, if he was ever going to start--
(a phone rings) Oh hey, it's—

ALSO ME
Yeah, we hate her.

ME
Send to voicemail.

Fuck. I wish there was someone to talk to. How come nobody ever calls me? Except, like, my mom.

ALSO ME
I mean, there's me, but...

ME
Yeah. No, I'm sorry, I didn't mean it like that.
Why does my head hurt? Everything always hurts. Am I getting sick?

ALSO ME
You're probably dehydrated.

ME
Oh. Yeah, you're probably right.
Can you get me some water?

ALSO ME
Can't, we would have to get out of bed.

ME
Well. I mean…who really needs water, right?
Hey. I'm sorry this play isn't better. It's all I really have the energy for.

"Wednesday, 1:07 PM," by Marisa Carr. Created alone in my apartment, in bed, on day 65 of isolation at 1:07 PM.

Saw things I imagined
I saw things I imagined
I saw things I imagined
I saw things I imagined
I saw things I imagined
Things I imagined
Things I imagined
Things I imagined
Saw things I imagined
I saw things I imagined
I saw things I imagined
I saw things I imagined
I saw things I imagined
Things I imagined
Things I imagined
Things I imagined

Taking on, taking on the lie
Taking on, taking on the lie
Taking on the lie.

← *"Listening to," by Jaime Castañeda. Things I Imagined by Solange. May 13, 2020.*

Coffee
Cats & Boots
a boost

EAT ME. I DON'T MIND.

Flash
Flood
TEARS

emotional support
chocolate splodge
spider

...
Still alone
...
Siri, hello
Hello
What day is it?
It's Friday, May 15th 2020
Should I get out of bed
Interesting question
Siri, I'm lonely.
I'm sorry to hear that. I'm here if you want to talk.
Tell me something interesting
I'm really more of a listener
Will you talk to me about something? Anything?
I don't have an answer for that. Is there something else I can help with?
I want you to change the subject and find something new to talk about.
Here are some things I found on the web.
You said I can talk to you and now you're not talking to me you just wanna do a web search
what kind of relationship is that!
But...I'm talking now.
Siri, get a grip
I'm not sure I understand.
I have to break up with you.
I don't understand "I have to break up with you.:" But I could search the web for it.
Ugh. Just beatbox.
Boots and cats and boots and cats and boots and cats and boots... I can do this all day... cats and boots
and cats and boots and cats and boots and cats and boots and cats and boots and cats and boots and
cats and boots and cats and boots and cats and boots and cats and boots and cats and boots and cats
and boots and cats and boots and cats and boots and cats and boots and cats and boots and cats and
boots and cats and boots and cats and boots and cats and boots and cats and boots and cats and boots
and cats and boots and cats and boots and cats and boots and cats and boots and cats and boots and
cats and boots and cats and boots and cats and boots and cats and boots and cats and boots and cats
and boots and cats and boots and cats and boots and cats and boots and cats and boots and cats and
boots and cats and boots and cats and boots and cats and boots and cats and boots and cats and boots
and cats and boots and cats and boots and cats and boots and cats and boots and cats and boots and
cats and boots and cats and boots and cats and boots and cats and boots and cats and boots and cats
and boots and cats and boots and cats and boots and cats and boots and cats and boots and cats and
boots and cats and boots and cats and boots and cats and boots and cats and boots and cats and boots
and cats and boots and cats and boots and cats and boots and cats and boots and cats and boots and
cats and boots and cats and boots and cats and boots and cats and boots and cats and boots and cats
and boots and cats and boots and cats and boots and cats and boots and cats and boots and cats and
boots and cats and boots and cats and boots and cats and boots and cats and boots and cats and boots

Wine
Fog...
rolling in.

*"Love In the Time of Covid," by Jo Cattell.
Shelter in place with only Siri for company.
Friday May 15th, 2020.*

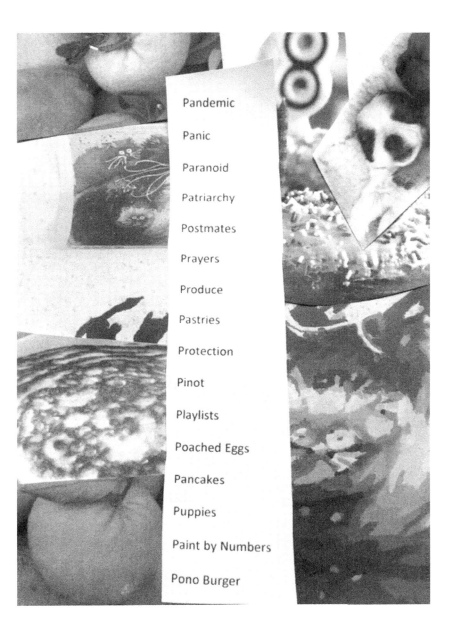

Pandemic

Panic

Paranoid

Patriarchy

Postmates

Prayers

Produce

Pastries

Protection

Pinot

Playlists

Poached Eggs

Pancakes

Puppies

Paint by Numbers

Pono Burger

"Privilege," by Jennifer Chambers. A musing on the "diversity" of quarantine. April 12, 2020.

Times I said I love you today

To my older son: 30

To my younger son: 30

To my dog: 29

To my husband: 1

*these are estimates, but close-ish to the truth. Or maybe I made them up completely. Or maybe this shows that I think I'm a better mom than I am and that I maybe think I'm a worse wife than I am. Or maybe I'm failing at both. Or succeeding? But maybe
I'll forgive myself today
because it's my fucking day.

"Mother's Day Fog," by Jackie Chung. May 10, 2020.

You are invited to celebrate the marriage of
Carmela Corbett & William Graham

THE VICAR
Do you William, take Carmela to be your wife, to have and to hold from this day forward, for better or for worse, for richer, for poorer, in sickness and in health, to love and to cherish; from this day forward until death do you part?

WILL
I do!

THE VICAR
Do you Carmela, take William to be your husband, to have and to hold from this day forward, for better or for worse, for richer, for poorer, in sickness and in health, to love and to cherish; from this day forward until death do you part?

CARMELA
I do!

Carmela Cynthia Corbett
Wife

William Robert Graham
Husband

"Wedding in the time of COVID-19," by Carmela Corbett. Conceived by a frustrated bride-to-be. May 22, 2020.

Room

Go to your room
And think about what you've done
What you haven't done
What you would have done
Could have done
And will do
And remember when we used to hold hands
What a fun hundred years that was
What you should do
They will need our help so soon
Very soon
But today nobody needs you
So just
Go to your room

Last modified: Mar 21, 2020

"Room," by Adam D. Crain. Written in my room, seemed non-essential. March 21, 2020.

"The Power of ceremony is it marries the mundane to the sacred."
    -Robin Wall Kimmerer, *Braiding Sweetgrass*

Like theater. Almost. If you squint.

← *"All Plays Are Prayers," by Cusi Cram.
Altars created March 17–May 17, 2020.*

I have been thinking about freedom.
I have thinking about the Bronx.
I have been thinking about the Zoo.

Every Wednesday, from ages 9 to 13, if I wasn't at the library, I was at the Zoo. I moved with purpose through the African Plains to the Big Cat enclosure. What a smell. It wasn't just the urine, but the grief, the loneliness. There was one snow leopard that I always went to see, because she seemed the saddest. She sprawled at the bottom of her cage, one paw hanging through the metal bars. I yearned to touch that paw, but settled for imitation. I hung my hand over the safety rail, trying to mimic her abandon. Then we'd lock tear-filled eyes.
But this is only the first stop.

The last stop brings me to the Great Apes. I see myself in the orangutan, so I always end here. There were no beautiful scenic enclosures when I first went to the Zoo. Back in the day, there was only metal and sadness. But when I escaped from the South Bronx to this magical animal place, I felt free. I felt safe. The walk to the zoo and back would be filled with bullies, gangs, ambulances and fire engines. Glass breaking. The word "spic" spit onto the concrete, crept inside my head—but sitting with my Orangutan, I felt peace. I was a writer. An inventor. A thinker. I could have my own thoughts and write them in my own notebook—that no one would try to tear from my arms today. Not today. She and I would stare at one another and share our despair. I still see her. In my mind's eye.
I see you.

"It's free on Wednesdays..." by Migdalia Cruz. On Day 62 of hiding from a microscopic organism that has already probably found me. May 14, 2020.

5/10/2020

Call of duty
(a play about the false notion of equivalency)

→ 2m, 2f
→ African janitor who was once a renowned doctor back in his country gets recruited by the US gov't to go back to work because there's a shortage of doctors now with covid-19
↓
and he also specializes in viruses and pandemics

scene 1
→ empty office building being cleaned & disinfected
→ only see the cart w/ supplies
→ Alberto enters, mopping
→ we see him clean for a while
→ Magdelena Ruiz, a gov't official from the CDC, enters
→ watches him
→ she introduces herself, it's all official sounding
→ he doesn't know what she wants with him
→ she makes the proposal for him to go to DC with her to work as a doctor again
→ he is shocked, jaded, says they have the wrong man
→ but she says no it's him they want because of his rep in his country
→ she makes promises
→ he sees a new life in front of him, maybe things will be different, better, if he steps in & can help.
→ he agrees

scene 10
→ empty office building being cleaned & disinfected
→ only see the cart w/ supplies
→ Alberto enters, mopping
→ we see him clean for a while
→ End

Moral of this story? Institutional racism has not disappeared "in the time of covid"! I will not tailor my stories. Write what you write. Speak up and out always.

more scenes maybe he saves the world? maybe things will be better for him.

PD

*"the only pandemic play i would ever write,"
by Francisca Da Silveira. Created while
caffeinating and watching celebrities
perform viral monologues in their nice
houses. May 10, 2020.*

APRIL SIXTH 327

She would have rambled on indefinitely on both sides of the subject if Nancy had not broken away.

When Nancy went into the house the tin-pan sound of the old piano and the throaty huskiness of Mary Mae Gates's voice were filling the Sunday silence with, "There is a green hill far away." Miss Ann, her face set in grim lines of stoicism, came out of the old library where Judge Baldwin had read "The Classmate" to the children on long ago Sunday afternoons. Miss Ann said Rilla had a headache and added pleasantly that, what with the air being so polluted with vocal artillery, it was a wonder she didn't have complete paralysis instead. Nancy would not allow Miss Rilla to be called, but she asked if Warner Field might come down for a moment. So Miss Ann called him and Warner came down. The first thing that came to him on the landing was how very little the weather was affecting Nancy. Her slim boyish body in its modish gown and close fitting hat looked cool, her whole appearance unruffled.

She looked up and laughed while he was still on the stairs. "You're not rid of me, yet, Warner," she called. "Am I not a bold maiden to chase you to your lair?" She had to be gay and natural before Miss Ann. "I wonder if you will come out and haul me in to the six-fifteen? Mattie has had a carload of people . . . two layers deep . . . arrive for supper and she will be serving it just at that time. So I thought you would do it for me instead of Walt."

Warner would, of course, although there went through him the swift fear of the bitter-sweetness of having to tell her good-by again.

Nancy said good-by to Miss Ann. Miss Ann said good-by in that constrained way of hers, shaking hands rigidly. "I hope you will always remember me kindly," she said stiffly.

← *"Untitled," by Mashuq Deen. May 18, 2020.*

I'm in a furniture store but it's actually a cupcake shop. There are free samples everywhere. I eat one. I ask a saleswoman how she's doing and she says she's reeling from Portland. Because in Portland, the cupcake shop had their worst case of food poisoning customers yet. It was brutal. I look at her. "Should I have eaten that sample?" She shrugs.

Fiona Apple is my writing teacher—a visiting professor. We're in the student-teacher lounge, and she spills coffee on herself because there's a hole in the pot. I find paper towels in a cupboard under the sink. She tells me she's finally figured out our homework assignment. I wonder, idly, if we'll ever do karaoke together as a class. Will Fiona like my voice?

There is a fire or explosion and people are running into various businesses along a commercial strip for cover. I run too, although I don't know why we're running and missed the explosion entirely.

A play of mine is having a production at a college. My mom is the director. I'm worried—does she have any experience? But she's done her research. "We're going to be using the Architecture of Space," she says. It's a concept coined by some Eastern European man she quotes. Several actors nod, excited. These are actors who don't realize that she is my mom.

I live in a little house in LA with a bunch of roommates. There's a bike path right outside the door. My sister and her husband are about to visit and right before they arrive, the house gets trashed. I'm angry, and make a scene in the kitchen. Do I say, "Listen up assholes?" I want everyone to Venmo me so we can treat them to a hotel room for the night. But my sister is pregnant, and she has to rush to the hospital. When she returns a day later, the baby is already a toddler—with curly hair and a little knit hat and a whole personality. She is adorable. My sister seems happy. Everything, for the moment, is simple.

← *"Anyone Else Having Vivid Dreams Lately?," by Steph Del Rosso. Trying to remind myself I can still be creative— at least while I'm sleeping. April 9–May 2, 2020.*

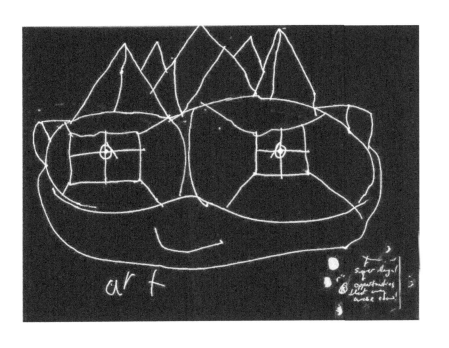

← *"Illegal Art," by Kristoffer and Leo Diaz. Traced shoe turned into a face then inverted with some scribbly notes from a conversation in a playwriting class. May 9, 2020.*

Are those jokes?
of course if want this I want

George Cram Cook, 1918:

Seven of the Provincetown Players are in the army or working for it in France, and more are going. Not light-heartedly now, when civilization itself is threatened with destruction, we who remain have determined to go on next season with the work of our little theatre. It is often said that theatrical entertainment in general is socially justified in this dark time as a means of relaxing the strain of reality, and thus helping to keep us sane. This may be true, but if more were not true—if we felt no deeper value in dramatic art than entertainment—we would hardly have the heart for it now. One faculty, we know, is going to be of vast importance to the half-destroyed world—indispensable for its rebuilding—the faculty of creative imagination. That spark of it which has given this group of ours such life and meaning as we have is not so insignificant that we should not let it die. The social justification which we feel to be valid now for makers and players of plays is that they shall help keep alive in the world the light of imagination. Without it the wreck of the world that was cannot be cleared away and the new world shaped.

"1918," by Julie Felise Dubiner. May 12, 2020.

"Untitled," by Erik Ehn. The images are cut-ups from a bunch of dollar comic books. The zigzag pattern comes from "Dance in Noh" by Monica Bethe and Karen Brazell. May 24, 2020.

Fight my sister.

Fight for your life.

I would do it for you if I could. I cannot. I cannot touch you. I cannot visit you except on a screen and now we all know how incredibly inadequate that is.

Fight.

Fight for your life or you will lose it.

I know it has been 40 days on the ventilator. I cannot imagine what that feels like inside your body. I understand why today you wanted to stop.

But fight.

For the first 20 days as the 11am update loomed I got sick inside, "Is this the day they tell us you died? That it is already over. That I have been eating oatmeal and complaining about my face mask fogging my sunglasses when I go out into a sun that you will never see again."

But you woke up. You smiled. You said your back hurt. You asked for ice cream. All without a voice because you don't have one because of the vent, the endless vent.

You gave me hope.

You have survived so much. Covid can not be the one that takes you. It's absurd.

Fight.

I promise I will not make you call my husband to tell me something because I never answer my phone. No matter how busy I am I will rejoice when I see it is your call because I get to hear your voice.

Fight.

Fight.

I need you to fight.

"a monologue to my sister because she can't have a dialog," by Larissa FastHorse. Written on the day she no longer wanted to fight, 5/5/20.

"a monologue to my sister because she can't have a dialogue," by Larissa FastHorse. Written on the day she no longer wanted to fight. May 5, 2020.

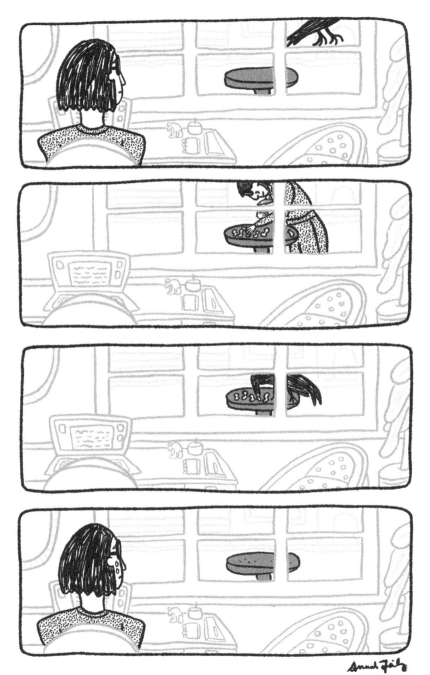

← *"Waiting for a Crow," by Annah Feinberg. A failed attempt at interspecies friendship. May 9, 2020.*

He wants to get out.
He craves the woods,
and he misses her.
But they would not approve.
"Not safe," they'd say.
"Against the rules," they'd say.
So, like most afternoons,
he slips out the *side* door.
He does *not* go to his car.
He walks around back,
over the footbridge,
across the meadow,
into the trails of the preserve
to their secret meeting spot.
He sees her car from the distance.
And her silver hair.
She sees the sun shining on his bald head.
They get close enough to touch fingertips
if they stretched out their arms.
But they don't do that.
They walk,
two widowers in the preserve,
behind the senior living complex.

"Preserve," by Liz Frankel. For my beloved 86-year-old step-father, whose charming story I've enjoyed sharing in these dark times, and the 81-year-old woman who has brought him happiness in recent years. May 9, 2020, the day before Mother's Day.

THIS IS BEING WRITTEN
ONTHE BACK
OF A PAGE

FROM A SCRIPT
OF A PLAY
THAT I WAS IN AT
SOHO REP LAST FALL

MY SON ALSO USED IT TO
WRITE DOWN HIS ONLINE LEARNING
SCHEDULE FOR THE DAY

WORDS
ON BOTH SIDES OF THE PAGE

NOW I'M USING IT
TO WRITE
ARTISTIC MUSINGS
i.e.
THEATRE
FOR A WORLD
WITHOUT THEATER

IT'S JUST WORDS

MONKEYS COULD HAVE WRITTEN IT
OR HAMLET
AND CERTAINLY WITH BETTER HANDWRITING

IT'S LIKE READING
LOU REED'S LYRICS
AS POETRY

IT SHOULD BE EXACTLY THE SAME
BUT IT'S DULL AND DISAPPOINTING
FOR BOTH OF US

← *"Words Words Words (or Both of Us)," by Gibson Frazier. Theatre without theater. May 27, 2020.*

Due to the spread of COVID-19 all Bella Figura stores will be closed until further notice. However, we are accepting orders have samples available and can be contacted at hello@bellafigura.com or 866-699-6040.

Due to the Covid-19 emergency for safety of all our employees and customers Chocolateria will be open from 10:00 AM to 6:00 PM. All sales will be take out until further notice. Thanks for your support. We are all in this together. Be safe Rosie, Michol Anthony.

CUSTOMER NOTICE
TAKEOUT/DELIVERY ONLY

Blue Bottle Coffee
Do your Part and Take Care
We Will See You Soon

Thank you for coming to Blue Bottle. To help slow the spread of COVID-19 as of March 16th, all US Blue Bottle Cafes are temporarily closed. Our baristas and all US cafe teams are taking care of themselves at home and we encourage you to do the same. Rest assured we are maintaining full rates of pay and health benefits for all staff. Above all, to meet the challenge of these uncertain times, we must take good care of each other. We look forward to welcoming you back as soon as we can. To learn more or order coffee online visit bluebottlecoffee.com to get the latest updates follow us on Instagram @bluebottle.

OUR MAIN PRIORITY IS TO KEEP OUR GUESTS AND ASSOCIATES AS SAFE AS POSSIBLE.

To ensure the safety of our guests and associates and do our small part for the community our **European Wax Center** has decided to temporarily close as a preventative measure in response to COVID-19 concerns. This is not a decision we take lightly. We apologize for any inconvenience this may cause and appreciate your patience at this time

Please be considerate and **give each other space** while shopping!!
Welcome we are open we are deemed an **essential business**

Flora

Cuomo,
During these days and speaking with our friends and clients we understanding more and more how difficult this situation is and will be for everyone, and not just us in the restaurant business. Therefore, once home in Red Hook, we have decided to close all our menu prices and change them accordingly in order to be able to take into consideration people's hardships during this time. We not only wish that our clients support the business, we would like to also support them, by serving them quality food and at the same time making it more reasonable. This is not a time to make "business" and think individualistically, but we need to band together, so that soon we can all start up again, stronger than before. OK so after this blah blah blah poem we're going to adjust the prices for all our menu items and from NOW ON prices are available for PICK UP ORDERS and already adjusted on SEAMLESS. You can pay less. but WE LOVE YOU MORE!

Unabbraccio!

PINKBERRY

We are temporarily modifying various service procedures to reduce touchpoints and cross-contact to help reassure you, our valued guest, that your safety is our top priority. Out of an abundance of caution, we have temporarily stopped all product sampling in our restaurants.

We apologize for any inconvenience

Dear Park Slope community,

Due to the ever evolving COVID-19 virus and safety we are changing our store hours for this week listed below

Friday 3/20/2020 2PM-5PM
Saturday 3/21/2020 2PM to 5PM

We will do our best to meet your needs. We apologize for any inconvenience this might cause. Starting next Monday March 23rd 2020, we will be temporarily closed until further notice. We will update our store hours when we were able to. Thank you for all your love and support over the years Please be well and stay safe! New United Laundry & Dry Cleaning

Mallory Y Rutledge MYR Inc. Face Skin Body

To all my "friends," Due to the virus I do have to close this studio. If you wish or need any refills I can make deliveries, just call or email be well and safe **XO** Mallory

"Conspiracy," by Matt Freeman. Found text, signs in shop windows. Park Slope, Brooklyn NY. March 22 & May 14, 2020.

Yesterday my husband and I went for a real hike **[Insert picture of wilderness here]** for the first time in a long time.

He spotted a pinecone on the ground **[Insert picture of pinecone here]**. He said, "We should grab one. Take it home."

What I thought was: "Don't you fucking touch that thing with your hands that also touch me."

What I said was..........................

"JOHN **PRINE**CONE

And then I asked...

"Too soon?"

Like some kind of asshole.[1]

"Huh. Yeah." He responded. "Too soon." ....We both love John Prine.

And then I said................PATSY **CLINE**CONE?[2]

> We took two pinecones home and discussed using them to become internet celebrities, which is not anything either of us wants. At least, it wasn't in our vows **[Insert wedding picture here]**. But things change. *People change. Hairstyles change. Interest rates fluctuate.*[3]

■■

That's the way that the world goes round / You're up one day, the next you're down / It's a half an enchilada[4], you think you're gonna drown / That's the way that the world goes round.

"Please Write the Footnotes," by Edith Freni. Created in lieu of miniature western wear, after a hike in a facemask, circa the end times. May 10, 2020.

```
instance_create (0, 0, rem);

// Shit. It's happening again. //

room_goto (stage);

// I haven't acted in years, and yet I keep finding myself here. //

instance_create (300, 600, audience);

// The old summer stock, housed in the junior college auditorium. //
// Twelve hundred seats, a person sitting in each one. //

instance_create (500, 1000, elizabeth);

// I remember her. Very sweet. A great dancer. //
// Oh shit, am I going to have to dance? //

show_message ("ELIZABETH: What sort of hat would Mrs. Hackl like?");

// What show is this? Clearly some quaint musical. //
// "Mame"? Am I in "Mame"? //

show_message ("ELIZABETH: What sort of hat would Mrs. Hackl like?");

// I instantly forget every line from every show I was ever in. //
// Is that a problem? Like, an early warning for something? //

show_message ("ELIZABETH: What sort of hat would Mrs. Hackl like?");
audio_play_sound (audience_cough, 30, true);

// Do something. //

if show = "Mame"
        {show_message ("Why Auntie Mame, how nice to see you!")}
else ();

// Elizabeth stares at me. I've somehow forgotten how to talk. //
// The show is clearly not "Mame". //

audio_play_sound (audience_murmur, 600, true);
show_message ("ELIZABETH: ... Is there a Mrs. Mackl?");

// I have to say something. //

if mrs_mackl = "True"
        {show_message ("Yes, and she's a Danish immigrant.")}
else if mrs_mackl = "False"
        {show_message ("Nope, I'm super single.")};

// Nothing's happening. Why can't I talk? //

audio_play_sound (audience_booing, 1200, true);
show_message ("ELIZABETH: Jesus Christ!");

// I'm so sorry. //

with elizabeth instance_destroy();

// I can do this. //
// Even with Elizabeth gone, I can still save the show. //
// I just have to speak. //
// Just ... speak! //
// I open my mouth ... //

with rem instance_destroy();
```

"Actor's Nightmare," by Jeremy Gable. Written in GameMaker Language. May 13, 2020.

Shopping List

- fettucini ~~TO DO~~ Pasta
  (Small ~~shells~~ ~~cfrogretti~~)
- shallots - ~~2~~ - 1 Red onion
- Bell Peppers - green - 2 - red - 2
- 1 pint heavy cream
- 1 qt. whole milk
- 2 heads broccoli florets
- Iceberg lettuce
- cucumber
- Tomatoes - Plum
- parsley
- Carrots & tops
- fuji apples -
- 2 - 16 oz cans Tomato sauce
  or - 1 - 30 oz can
- Sargento - fontina cheese
  " - shredded cheddar cheese

Gorgonzola cheese

Canadian bacon
Chicken cutlets   TO DO

Dijon Mustard
Deli - low sodium Ham
    Alpine Swiss Cheese

"Priorities," by Joanna Glum (with Elaine).
A grandmother's shopping list in lockdown.
May 15, 2020.

The baby is awake
after a 40-minute
nap.
Did we put her
down too late? Too
early?
The dogs were
barking. Did they
wake her up?
I took a shower.
I clipped my
toenails. My
sweater smells like
bubblegum.
I can't imagine
why. I have not
had or seen any.
I have only been
outside and inside.
The sweater
bacteria must
make a sweet
scent. Do they do
that on purpose?

To what end? What do bacteria know about how humans love?
When someone says, the virus is smart, what do they mean? When my partner says, the virus is smart, does she mean it will kill her? Does she mean in the hospital it will track her sweet blood, the fresh nursing license, the doctoral program in peds, Type I diabetes and the ten-month-old baby who has only just this week discovered a soft toy can be loved, can become a friend, a soft toy, a four-inch kangaroo finger puppet can accompany one in hand as one crosses the floor, as one drags one's body over thresholds, as one passes
from inside to outside
from risk to risk?

"She's going to go back to work at the hospital," by Emma Goidel. May 11, 2020.

"Day 60: EQ Pop Quiz!" by Jacqueline Goldfinger and Rachel Goldfinger. Pick One Answer: A B C D E F G H I J K L ((Do you feel insufficient yet?)) M N O P Q R S T ((How about now?)) U V W X Y Z ((You're still standing? Let's take it to Level 2!)) AA BB CC DD EE FF GG HH II JJ KK LL MM NN O... O.. O. o ((You Fail. Good Girl. Congratulations! Reset: 6am.)) May 10, 2020.

← *"catastrophic thinking," by Isaac Gómez (photo credit: Rashaad Hall). First enforced mask day in Los Angeles, Melrose District — post-grocery shopping. April 4, 2020.*

TO
  BE
    IS
  BEING
    IS
      HARD
      HARDLY
  BEING
    BEGIN
     BEGAN
      BEAN
       BAN
        N.B.
         B
          C D E F G   H   I J K L   M N
                                      O
                                     P Q
                                       R
                                       S
                                       T
                                       U
                                       V
                                        W
                                         X
                                         Y
                                         BEEN
                                         BE.   N

Until I was 10, I thought the term was HUMAN BEAN

← *"Forrest / Tree / Sound," by Tasha Gordon-Solmon. I made this in color but you're seeing it in black and white. May 16, 2020.*

LAVINIA sits, alone.

The sound of rain beginning to fall.

End of play.

"Buried Alive," by Kirsten Greenidge. An affirmation for Kaitlyn, whose baby rarely sleeps. May 15, 2020.

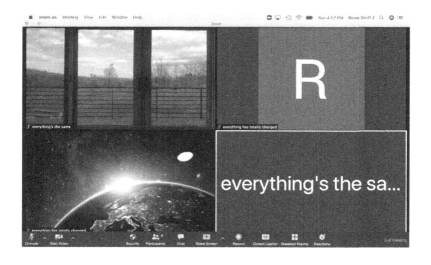

← *"everything's the same/has totally changed," by Rinne Becker (aka Groff). Zoomed out. Sunday, May 10, 2020.*

Dear reader, you hold in your hand an entirely new theatrical experience. What is more glorious than the discovery of an entirely new art form, like an unlooked-for comet blazing in the empyrean! Behold!

The play you hold on your hand has a duration of forty-two days. It may be performed or enjoyed by anyone, of character or temperament, be they miserly or prodigal, rich or poor, young or old, born beneath the torrid zone or near the poles, provided that one inhabits a room. Admission to this play is free, making it ideal for an audience of moderate means. It is safe from disasters of any kind, perfect for any audience or actor who are sick, idle, unhappy, or weary.

Why forty-two days? I do not know. If it is too long for you, reader, it is not my fault that it is not shorter. Now, let the play begin.

Keep very close to the wall and trace its shape, counting the steps. Traverse a separate journey. And another. Travel back and forth across your room in as many ways as possible without ever repeating a route. Do you have an armchair? Take up your quarters therein. By the by, what a capital article of furniture an armchair is, and above all, how convenient to a thoughtful person! A good fire, some books and pens; what safeguards these against ennui! Allow the rays of the sun to play upon your curtains. See them come creeping, as the sun rises, all along the whitened wall. If there are elm-trees opposite your windows, watch them divide the sun-rays into a thousand patterns as they dance upon your bed. Have confused swallows taken possession of your roof? Do warbling birds people your elms? Listen to their twitter. Allow a thousand smiling fancies to fill your soul, and know that in the whole universe no being enjoys an awakening as delightful, as peaceful, as yours. Allow your soul to become disengaged from matter and let it travel alone as it pleases. Employ it to examine your animal self's progress. Allow it to prepare your breakfast, to slice and toast your bread, to make your coffee admirably.

Your efforts are useless. Sojourn here awhile. The Halt is irresistible.

Do not reproach me for the prolixity with which I narrate the details of your journey. When one performs Hamlet, *or* A Streetcar Named Desire, *the minutest particulars are carefully described. Upon this principle I resolve to speak of my dog, Rose, an amiable creature for whom I entertain sincere regard. We have lived together for six years, and there has never been any coolness between us, and if ever any little disputed have arisen, the fault has been chiefly on my side, and Rose has always made the first advances towards reconciliation. In the evening, if she has been scolded she withdraws sadly and* CURTAIN

"Play for One Person," by Jason Grote. May 27, 2020.

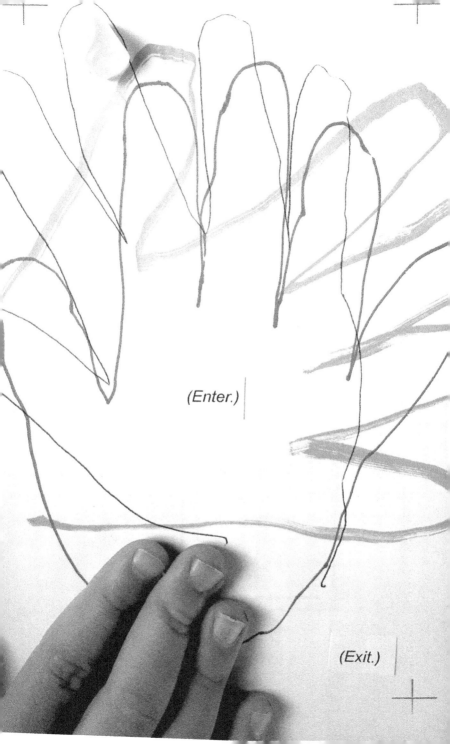

"Enter/Exit," by Lauren M. Gunderson. Created right before I had a Zoom meeting but promised him I'd build his Lego rocket ship if he let me trace his hand for this art project." 10:55am, May 11, 2020 in my upstairs office, San Francisco CA.

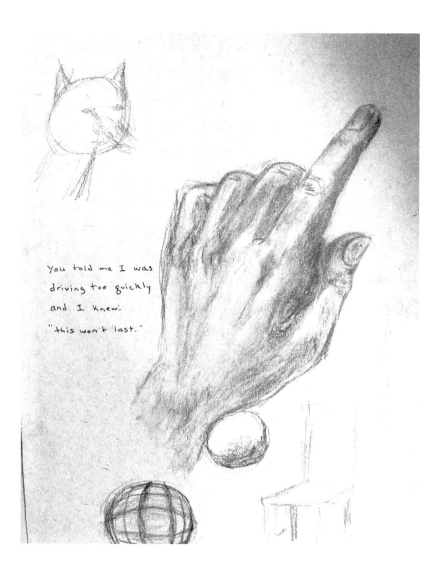

You told me I was
driving too quickly
and I knew:
"this won't last."

"This is Temporary," by Mary Elizabeth Hamilton. Created while in quarantine with my 9 year old. (We've been watching a lot of Youtube drawing classes.) May 17, 2020.

- ☐ bios / audio plays
- ☑ postcard stats → Rebecca W
- ☑ Consuelo / Izzy → B's personaje de libro
- ☐ Kayla's address / teacher appreciation <u>scones.</u>
- ☑ Weissberger / ward doc + ♡ to K.B.

~~████████████████████~~

- <u>Carework</u>
- <u>Fierce Femmes</u>
- <u>No One Is Too Small...</u>

- <u>The Yellow House</u>

        research / books

Interdependence

← *"are the worlds colliding or were they always already one world," by Adrien-Alice Hansel. Actual found object, to-do list. (Photo taken from the same computer I use to photograph every assignment my daughter refuses to do on her Chromebook.) May 8, 2020.*

theatre can't die
only people can

"an important message from our managing director," by Elizabeth Harper. Prop scythe with human skull and vertebrae. Taken at Santa Maria dell'Orazione e Morte, where theatre was performed by the dead for the spiritual edification of the living, 1763 to 1880. May 10, 2020.

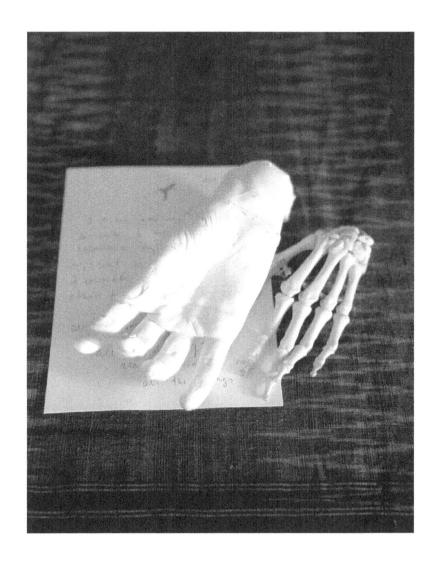

"What will I write before I die?" by Julie Hébert. The day before my 66th birthday, 37 days into lockdown. May 2020.

so the thing is
the theater wilderness
has a lot of grackles.
and they're all over
and you see them all the time
and they're rejections.
rejection grackles.
and then every so often there's
a strange opportunity hawk
and it's just sitting there eating the head
of a grackle and you're like
wtf who are you and it says
i am an opportunity hawk.

but now the world is weird
and there's no grackles or hawks
and we're gonna have to look for other birds.
like common yellowthroats
and eastern towhees
and house finches
and woodpeckers
and other birds whose meanings
are unclear.

birds that were maybe always around
but we never looked for
because we were busy
and all our glances were quick
so we only noticed the grackles and the occasional hawk.

so i think we're gonna have to content ourselves
with new birds
and miss the familiarity of grackles
and miss the welcomeness of hawks
and miss knowing what the fuck we were looking for
because the birds we knew are gone now
but we are still here.

"bird watching," by Justice Hehir. May 15, 2020.

COMMIT. COMMIT30 is actually the full name. It's this hot pink day planner. The planner comes with pages of stickers that say things like: "Best Life Ever" and "JOY!" - you're supposed to decorate each day with them. I was not planning to do that. But there's spaces for all kinds of time management and creative goal setting. Even, they suggest, for the inspired collage. If I don't have good time management skills to start with (I don't), I'm not sure how inspired collaging my day planner will remedy this, and the whole thing is kind of too much cheerful twee, but still this hot pink planner had been stalking me on Facebook since the New Year, and finally I buckled. It was probably just the color. My planner full of calls to daily self-actualization and focused, joyful(!) goal setting arrived maybe March 4th or 5th. Now it sits unused on my kitchen countertop, mocking me. I mean, I suppose I could write down my kids' Zoom class times in it. 10 am Story Time Zoom ("Joy!" sticker!). But it feels like overkill. My kids are not quite 4 and 5 1/2. They have one 30-minute Zoom class a week. Today my husband and I discuss that it's likely we will be home schooling them until at least Fall 2021. I can keep track.

For the past 63 days, I mean please understand me literally each and every one of them, I have ricocheted from one ridiculous psychosomatic ailment to the next. First it was my coccyx, my tailbone. Just the deepest ache, made me weep, nothing was helping. My mother-in-law tells me that my coccyx is my First Chakra. Ruler of community/finding one's tribe/security/safety/identity. Well, okay. I haven't nursed my kids in well over three years, but I get a painful blocked milk duct. (That one kind of writes itself, doesn't it.) There's a small freckle-like mole that appears on my left ankle. It's tiny, but dark. I worry. There's nothing to be done. There are no doctor appointments anymore. I put it out of my mind. My kids don't read yet. They're too young, of course. So it's not like they ever go off and read a book. They are amazing and coping miraculously and very young. We play all day. We try to slip in little stabs at something approximating "school." Andy is a filmmaker and composer. He is writing up a brilliant storm, upstairs in his office. He's easily got 4 new screenplays, ready to shoot. He is climbing the walls in his own way. I'm an actor so there's no work. Maybe theatre died? We're not sure. TV and Film will come back. It will be fine, people say, kind of like the porn industry; everyone will just wear masks, except for the actors. I play with my kids. I'm a Bad Pirate, a Bad Police Officer, a Maniacal Chicken who chases them around the endless loop of our kitchen. I worry about my ankle. I stare at it for two months. Finally I make a Tele-Health appointment. My dermatologist thinks it's nothing, but she wants to see it in person. They're opening back up again, tentatively, slowly - this week. May 12th, I can put on a mask and go in. Get in my car and drive 30 minutes and park and go into an office building -- it all seems impossible. I haven't driven a car, I haven't left my house beyond my neighborhood walk since quarantine began. But it's a dark freckle-mole. It's what I must do. I sit in her tiny office, with my mask and gloves on. I take off my shoe. So. So it's not there. This mole, which has been there every day, haunting me for the past two months, is suddenly and totally gone. I study all around my foot, for real I do this. Could it have moved?? Is it... on the *other* foot? Am I crazy? She informs me that it's just what she had suspected. A tiny internal hemorrhage (a bruise), that has rubbed off, because of the friction of my sock. Which I had started wearing in my crazy-pants way 24/7, because *it upset me* to look at the freckle-mole. My glasses are ill-fitting and keep sliding down over my mask and off my face, like 10 times, crashing to the floor of the doctor's office. And also the stairwell (can't take the elevator). And then onto the sidewalk out front *right in front of the trash can*. Everywhere they land is a minefield. I debate the risks of putting the glasses back on my face or driving home 30 minutes on the highway without my distance vision. I think we all know which I chose. And now I have broken my family's quarantine, to go to a big office building, brushing past more masked people at close range than I have seen since March 10th, in the middle of a global pandemic, driving — driving actually half-blind, and it wasn't even *there* because of my hysterical sock wearing. I mean, please know: I'm deeply grateful and overjoyed that it's nothing. (Joy! sticker!) And also, I am now taking anti-anxiety medication. It should kick in end of the month.

"Best Life Ever" by Laura Heisler. Written when I could, 5/14/20.

"Best Life Ever," by Laura Heisler. Written when I could. May 14, 2020.

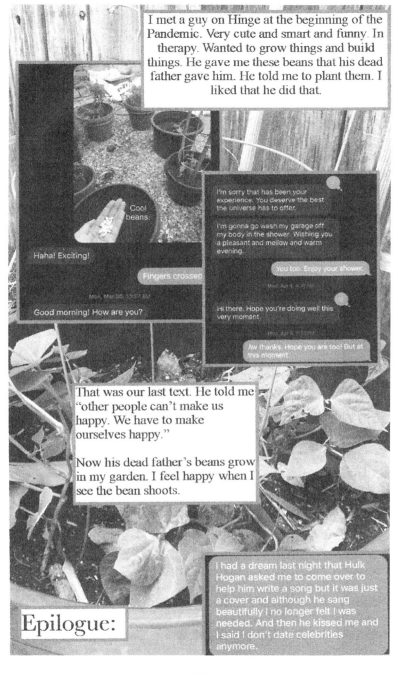

"seeking a lover who can do math," by Alex Henrikson. Made after a dream about falling in love with Hulk Hogan. May 11, 2020.

"Reason 52 Why We Have To Get Busy Writing New Stuff," by Deb Hiett. Quarantine Day 52. May 13, 2020.

My partner Jon and I put this whiteboard on our fridge on March 13, 2020, the day we first went into quarantine together. We update it daily.

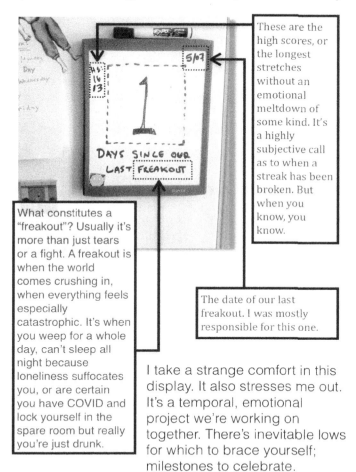

These are the high scores, or the longest stretches without an emotional meltdown of some kind. It's a highly subjective call as to when a streak has been broken. But when you know, you know.

What constitutes a "freakout"? Usually it's more than just tears or a fight. A freakout is when the world comes crushing in, when everything feels especially catastrophic. It's when you weep for a whole day, can't sleep all night because loneliness suffocates you, or are certain you have COVID and lock yourself in the spare room but really you're just drunk.

The date of our last freakout. I was mostly responsible for this one.

I take a strange comfort in this display. It also stresses me out. It's a temporal, emotional project we're working on together. There's inevitable lows for which to brace yourself; milestones to celebrate.

"Fridge Report," by Daniel Hirsch (with contributions by Jonathan Cuevas). A photo and explanatory diagram of the author's daily freakout countdown routine. May 8, 2020.

**Interior apartment kitchen- dusk.
An Adult Daughter enters. Her Mother sits.**

MOM: What was that?
DAUGHTER: What was what?
MOM: That conversation.
DAUGHTER: What conversation?
MOM: The one you were just having with the super.
DAUGHTER: What about it?
MOM: You were flirting with him.
DAUGHTER: I was not.
MOM: He has a key, you know. You shouldn't be so friendly. He could come in and rape us.
DAUGHTER: Jesus, Mom.
MOM: I'm just sayin'.
DAUGHTER: What, you want me to be a bitch to him? He could just as easily come in and murder us.
MOM: Just keep your distance.
DAUGHTER: We could move. There are plenty of buildings with female supers.
MOM: Move? With my bad leg?
DAUGHTER: True.
(Silence)
MOM: Did you tip him this Christmas?
DAUGHTER: I was supposed to tip him?
MOM: Yes!
DAUGHTER: I don't have extra cash for that.
MOM: Well, it's too late now. Jesus. (Long Pause) I didn't tell you, but I've been experiencing pain on my right side.
DAUGHTER: What kind of pain?
MOM: Cancerous pain.
DAUGHTER: Just ignore it. It's probably nothing.

"Women Who Worry," by Lily Holleman. The day after dreaming Alex Jones stole her spinach salad. May 14, 2020.

He tenderly licks his butt, the pink skin, the soft white fur dampening against the black. He works his way to the base of his tail, then, like an acrobat in front of the judges, he stretches his back leg behind his head, tucks it in place with his neck, and laps at his inner thigh. He's quiet, composed, serene. This is peaceful. This is washing.

CAT
Ah-choo!

Some fur flies through the air. He continues his work, performing smack in the middle of the cold, tiled foyer, the space where all things connect. At 16, he has mastered his art form. I envy him. He seems apathetic that you're watching him so closely. He's not performing for you.

When his task is done, he folds himself together again. He stands and licks his lips.

CAT
Mmm

How satisfying it is to be clean again. There's nowhere to go, but cleanliness prevails.

He meanders to the couch, curls into a tight ball, and drifts away.

← *"Can cats really get coronavirus?" by Jess Honovich. Collaboration with Figaro. May 12, 2020.*

GUARDIAN Listen, are you going to visit me in my dreams?

Schedule is subject to change with fair notice by the instructor in class.

Date	Initial Class Schedule
Mar 12	EXAM #1 in class (bring green book)
Mar 16-20	SPRING BREAK
Mar 24	Unit 4: Argentina and Immersive Theater, Day 1 Entry point exercises Discuss history of late twentieth-century Argentina and the "Dirty War"
Mar 26	Immersive Theater, Day 2 Read before class: Play readings E In class: DR #8
March 31	CESAR CHAVEZ DAY – NO CLASSES TODAY
Apr 2	Immersive Theater, Day 3 Read for today: Critical articles on March 26 reading In class: DR #9 In class: Wrap-Up #4
Apr 7	Unit 5: Chile and Circular Dramaturgy, Day 1 Entry point exercises in studio DUE: Planning Work for Final Projects

(…Suddenly, a group of men burst in, hurling themselves at a person in the audience who is talking with someone else. This other person is for a second paralyzed with astonishment. Then shouting, he throws himself into the fray.)

"No set meeting time," by Scott Horstein. Created during finals week. Text at top of page from Ramón Griffero, <u>Midday Lunches or Petit Dejeuner du Midi in Your Desires in Fragments and Other Plays</u>, translated by Adam Versényi, Oberon Books, 2016, p.70. Text at bottom of page from Griselda Gambaro, <u>Information for Foreigners</u> in <u>Information for Foreigners: Three Plays</u>, edited, translated, and with an introduction by Marguerite Feitlowitz, with an afterword by Diana Taylor, Northwestern University Press, 1992, p.88. May 12, 2020.

A C T   I

said standing,
while looking out a window
shortly before sunset

We were walking up the cliffside, back to our car from the beach. As we began to cross the road, a helicopter roared by overhead, flying low, its rotors beating loudly, enveloping us in a wave of Doppler effect Surround Sound as it passed. Looking south, the shoreline stretched as far as the eye could see, the tallest buildings of Santa Monica and beyond just barely visible in the distance. Looking north, the beach became cliffs and more cliffs, the Pacific Coast Highway an asphalt ribbon lined with parked cars. *I remember this.* Motorcycles and helicopters, the crashing of the waves and the wind, gulls and other sea birds screeching as they glide in long arcs above us looking into the sea for fish. *At the end of the continent.* For one moment, the blink of an eye, really, I am overcome with vertigo, the feeling that things really *are* falling apart. Here we are *at the edge of a continent*, the end of history, what once were laws are now merely suggestions, all these people in close proximity and it is only a matter of time until the veneer of civility that keeps the chaos at bay disappears entirely. So, this is California. This is Los Angeles, 2018.

> *A country road. A tree.*
>
> *(what is) the end of acceleration?*
>
> *Evening.*
>
> *(giving up again).* Nothing to be done.

ACT II

the sky is a bright clear blue and the hum of busy-ness has receded but for the occasional helicopters. the creek runs clear. birdsong all day long. squirrels and possums and geese.

recited softly over a sleeping child:
there is a world within the world. there is a sound that is all sounds. there is time within time. everything is always being revealed and just as quickly hidden. look closely. listen closer. everything is waiting for you. everything is always exactly as it must be. there is no other world than this one. I will leave this here for you now to discover when you need it.

*"The End of Acceleration," by Andy Horwitz.
Upon the occasion of being awoken at
3:24am yet again, consumed by equal parts
peace and terror. May 18, 2020.*

←

the song is sad for itself it makes itself sad this song	*i wake up at 4am*
should be eviscerated in your opinion and mine but we're just sitting here	*i get out of bed*
living in it like that's enough it's not enough	*my downstairs neighbors are up*
it can't be enough this can't be what it means to have a whole life i need to know you think this song is also bad	*they play their bass guitars*
or at least this is not your favorite or maybe maybe this is	*all before-day long*
just	*into the next night*
your only song right now	*and i*
in which case okay we'll listen to it	*i come to love the*
together	*determined*
and that	*practice*
can be enough	*of their half-heard songs* *beating at the floorboards* *of this venue* *my home*

"the downstairs neighbor boys invited me over for a beer and i said no?" by Emma Horwitz. Created while my downstairs neighbors were out at the grocery, finally. May 20th, 2020.

THINGS I'VE SAID OR THAT HAVE BEEN SAID TO ME ON ZOOM
MINI SCENES

A: i went on tik tok cause i think that's where people find muses now.
B: everyone on there looks like bratz dolls.

A: she looks like charles manson.
B: that's cause she is.

A: no one on animal crossing has ocd.
B: except you.

A: do you want book suggestions?
B: that's okay.

A: the theme could be flowers. we could all write plays about flowers.
B: outer space is more interesting than flowers.

A: i haven't tried to bake bread yet.
B: i don't know how to properly cook chicken.

A: i keep having dreams. like weird, vivid dreams i'm not prepared for. mainly about needing to go back to highschool because i forgot to finish math class. but i'm not a teenager again, i'm just me, old and weird, sitting in math class. and everyone is dressed better than me, like-
B: like bratz dolls?

ARE YOU A OR B?

* my brother Henry drew these

← *"Things I've Said or That Have been Said to Me on Zoom: Mini Scenes," by Lily Houghton and her brother, Henry. May 10, 2020.*

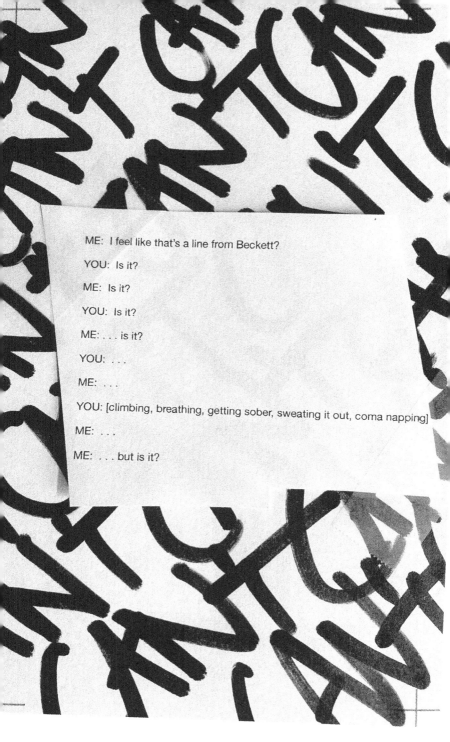

ME: I feel like that's a line from Beckett?

YOU: Is it?

ME: Is it?

YOU: Is it?

ME: . . . is it?

YOU: . . .

ME: . . .

YOU: [climbing, breathing, getting sober, sweating it out, coma napping]

ME: . . .

ME: . . . but is it?

"omg I do not know if this is 300 dpi brain inside out sending care my children are screaming," by Lindsay Brandon Hunter. May 15, 2020.

lights up
sunrise
moonrise
breadrise
reprise
surprise
surmise
earthrise

sunset
moonset
reset
regret
forget
strike the set
earthset
end of play

← *"Geological Time," by Kristin Idaszak in collaboration with Shane Kelly. This is a durational piece performed over 12 billion years, beginning with the birth of the earth 4.5 billion years ago and ending with the death of the sun in 7.5 billion years. May 17, 2020.*

This is the story of my mom
And how she goes to the hospital every other week
Even though the world is on fire
Even though the hospital is the scariest place to be in a world on fire
This is also the story of the Cake Lady and the Gentleman From India
These are the names my mom has given them
My mom calls them her chemo buddies
They've sat together for over a year
Sometimes the Gentleman From India dozes off
Sometimes the Cake Lady does Sudoku
Mainly, though, they talk
My mom tells them about her grandson

She tells them about his exploits in baseball
The walk off home run that turned the game around
The way he swung his bat and how the ball soared over the fence
And how much she misses watching him play
And how he found our cat Kevin who we thought was lost forever
It was a miracle, she says, and I don't even believe in miracles
And how her grandson gets taller every day
And how he taught her a funny dance from a video he saw online
I'll show you, she says
And so she does
Sitting in her chemo chair, she recreates each move
Hands and arms in motion, careful of the tube leading to her port
Step by step, she teaches them
My mom, the Cake Lady, and the Gentleman From India
Three strangers dancing together in a world on fire

"3 Strangers," by Naomi Iizuka. Dedicated to my mom on Mother's Day 2020. May 10, 2020.

because what else can you do but look to the stars because eye contact in public means something slightly different now because you might need to help someone feel seen because you might need to just get in the car and drive because I will make an exception for you because on Emerson I held your broken voice to my ear because just today the buds started to blossom because the vocabulary has shifted gradually over time because breath is vital because I'm afraid I won't be able to use up this produce before it goes bad because I don't want to be wasteful because you might need to teach yourself on the fly because you might want to work hard for an idea that is mortal because where can a person get rolls of quarters for laundry these days anyway because how does one reconcile fabric versus cardboard because I stared at these groceries wondering if I should wash them because "you can't food a virus" because on Wednesday decisions felt harrowing but by Thursday they were obvious because prior to the official mandate he came over with three kinds of cake to help us think it through because certain dreams will stick upon waking and inform how you behave that day because ancestors clearly are trying to speak to you through clocks because the psychic unprompted told me I probably won't die soon because sometimes even mild exposure to sunlight changes an outcome because you once wrote "bold and dangerous" because I said "no" then later "yes" because eighteen months later your "yes" became "no" because nothing lasts forever because I'm only beginning to digest certain facts because thirteen months later the cracks became unavoidable because even though I didn't know who I was then you taught me how to build routines because even though you were looking in another direction I taught you how to open time-sensitive envelopes because even though people survive worse all the time twilight is cyclonic because sense memory because we are still beginners because we're so tender because we're not fucking up because nothing will be the same after because now everyone is a phoenix because there's only one sign left because you'll always remember who you've lost in the morning because you'll always remember who you touched during the pandemic

- 161 -

← *"Apologies for My Delayed Response," by Rachel Jendrzejewski. Seven weeks past the deadline and counting. May 8, 2020.*

← *"A cactus. The future (metaphorically?). My day-to-day life (metaphorically and literally). Resilience. Adaptation. Beauty. What I wish I could be but am not. I am the worst at making titles. Trying to find acceptance. How is nature so fucking beautiful?" by Kate Jopson. My only job left in COVID-world is making videos about cacti and succulents for my brother's nursery. May 13, 2020.*

← *"Pillow with a Face," by Lila Rose Kaplan and Hailey (age 5). May 2, 2020.*

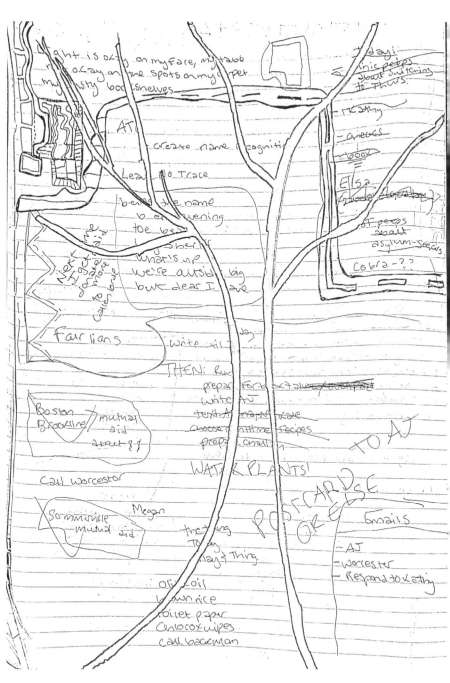

"for the trees this spring is the same as any other," by MJ Kaufman. By the way this is a real page from my notebook created over the course of a week from May 15 – May 22, 2020.

"I Find Myself Drawing Old People Again, Suddenly," by Lucas Kavner. A conversation I remember having in high school, as I find myself constantly doodling old people again, suddenly. May 12, 2020.

"A Space To Make - West Adams," by Lisa Kenner Grissom. An adventure in movement during Covid, in collaboration with choreographer Alexandra Shilling. April 26, 2020.

So far I've killed only one houseplant.
[Abandoned plays]
"No." "No." "No." "Maybe." "No."

Baking. Cooking. Ignoring emails.
[My Chipotle apocalypse play, now too timely]
"Thank you."

Dead car battery.
[*MAY 39th*, the play I wrote 14 years ago about living in isolation pods after a pandemic]
"I'm fine."

Sharing buttermilk and onions.
[No one wants that play]
"Is she still on a ventilator?"

2 years of isolation from a brain injury.
[I don't even want that play]
"Let me find the link."

Any crying is usually brief. So is any sleep.
[I keep whispering "amphitheaters"]
"Stay safe."

*"Estrangement," by Callie Kimball.
Sheltering in solitude. May 16, 2020.*

A Short List of Things I've Dramaturged* That Aren't Plays Since I Can No Longer Bring Myself to Read Plays, Apparently

- My closet
- Our fridge
- My family's Mother's Day zoom call
- My best friend's job search

A Short List of Things That Would Benefit From Some Rigorous Dramaturgical Investigation If Only I Had The Energy

- That other closet
- That shelf in the bathroom
- My career aspirations
- All those plays in my inbox

*No one can quite agree on a definition of dramaturgy—a debate broke out on the Literary Managers and Dramaturgs of the Americas listserv this week, and Word is giving me angry red squiggles under the word "dramaturged"—and certainly what I have done to my closet and fridge and family zoom call bears little similarity to what I did to *Phaedra's Love* in my college dramaturgy class, but what I mean to say here is that I have dug into these things, I have ripped them apart, I have asked a series of questions of them, I have found connections and meaning (for myself and for others), I have advised discarding what isn't working (hence the pile of clothes, once in my closet, now on my floor, because there is nowhere to donate clothes right now; I have killed my darlings but I am stuck with the bodies), I have questioned some more, I have thrown my hands up in frustration, I have re-engaged and ultimately been grateful that I did.

"Two Short Lists," by Ramona Rose King. Written in the first burst of creativity in weeks. May 12, 2020.

"ride 'em cowboy," by Krista Knight. On the occasion of the git getting on. May 14, 2020.

rush of a stream
a white-washed barn
stone walls three hundred years old

daffodils that sprout in bouquets
conifers one hundred feet tall

air that's silly with minerals
water that tastes like dessert

the assiduous forest
constant sky
stars that always come through

I was saddened by all the deaths from the start
I am saddened by all the deaths today
I am saddened by all the deaths
what else is there?

still, in tandem, in the mountains, I've been restored to myself

"The Virus That Saved Me," by Andrea Kuchlewska. Made on the east side of Thorn Mountain in Jackson, New Hampshire. May 12, 2020.

WHEN WILL I
WHEN WILL WE
HOW WILL IT
I hope.
STOP BEGIN
AGAIN

I hope.

I hope.

← *"Curtain Call," by Jenni Lamb. Created as I searched for answers outside my home office window that faces a deteriorating building. May 17, 2020.*

Listen …
There's a secret that all little brown girls know …
In time, it won't always be as hard as it is now.
It won't … it won't.
You won't …
You won't always feel like the roots of a large oak tree fighting through rock and hard clay and cement just to quench your thirst.
You won't always feel odd, ugly, lonely, ashamed, and out of place.
You won't want any of this to end as much as you do now.
You won't …
Just wait …
Wait …
Please wait …
Because some day …
Some wonderful, ordinary, beautiful day …
You will look in the mirror and love the person staring back at you.
You will love her pain and anguish …
Her strength and courage.
Her optimism and belief in fighting for what is right and just.
You will love her and thank her for fighting with everything she had to stay alive and be here today.
You will … you will … you will.
Until then, oh beautiful little brown girl …
Until then, smile your brightest, open your eyes wide to world around you, get hopelessly lost in your imagination, and wear that red dress each and every Christmas until it no longer fits and has fallen apart at the seams.

← *"This I Promise You," a spoken word poem written through tears by Jacqueline E. Lawton. Written on a day she felt loved and beautiful and wished her younger self to know this day would come. May 16, 2020.*

THERE'S WALLY

Nikki (He/They)

Marian Gonzales (She/Her/HRH)

Julie Ouellette (She/They)

Chris (He/They)

Jer Adrianne Lelliott (She/They)

Jay Kuhns (He/They)

Wally (They/Them)

Ella Baker (She/Her/Hers)

MJ (They/Them/She/Her)

Vico (They/Him/She)

Provvidenza (They/Them)

← *"There's Wally!" by Jer Adrianne Lelliott & Julie Oullette. Queer affirmation in times of crisis. May 13, 2020.*

I have two alarms set
    9am wake up
    9pm stop eating
I ignore both
    sleeping until 10am or cuddling with Sebastian
    eating at 9pm because I'm stoned

HEY ANYTHING THAT WORKS TO FEEL JOY

← *"health," by Sarah Rose Leonard. Thought while gazing at a lemon tree. May 17, 2020.*

three weeks to the day, today and
I can no longer run
around this neighborhood
passing the streets
that sprout up like
weeds in my memory
all the houses my best friend lived in
(Copa de Oro)
the street that shares a name
with our friend's childhood dog
(Tucker Lane)

I suddenly remember
passing the library
the sweltering feeling
of impossibly long
summer days
old enough to know
there was more
whole worlds
just beyond reach
we did not yet have access to

for a flash, I'm confused to see toys
because everyone who lived here
grew up alongside me
and is now grown, and away
or back again
before I remember
that's not how it works

now,
I hear our neighbor's whistle
as it curves through
twilit streets
to tell me
it's time to come home

(a concept I've wrestled with
for so long
as much as one can wrestle
while knowing the answer
and fighting against it)

three nights now I can't sleep
you told me the summer after I left
you'd hear our cat crying
in the middle of the night
try to pull his little body up
from the bottom of the bed
like you did when he was a kitten
but of course, he wasn't there
he was with me
states away

but now, my roommate tells me
they are sending love
through the floorboards
so here in California
though my cats are in Brooklyn,
every time I stand
I will feel their love like roots
underneath me

but the surest way to get me to want something
is to pull away, and away

a few nights ago
a reoccurring dream, now
of a villa, sun-drenched
where my friends and I are safe
and have found our way together
a boy speaks the warnings of my heart:

I must accept the harm I've done
to those I've let love me
behind the castle-wall of my heart

I don't know how to be close, anymore

I'm trying

this morning,
I ran on the ocean
smiled at every single person I passed
specs of tar on the soles of my feet
cut my toe on a shell
keep going
foggy and gorgeous
the gloom
I thought: I could do this forever

but the surest way to get me to pull away
is to open your heart to me

and my horoscope today said **this is a time to**
figure out why you keep falling in love with people who are not
good for you. Human life is so delicate that a word from
someone you love can make you tremble.

but what is the difference between a word
and a touch

they'll close them all tomorrow
state-wide
and while I know
it's well-meaning
the press on my chest
the shrinking of an already shrunk world
confined for many hours of the day
to a screen in my palm
the panic as it
holds my lungs
breathe, and breathe again

to be free

"adapted from a poem titled 'free'," by Sofya Levitsky-Weitz. Written in the suburbs for the month of May. May 8, 2020."

(A spotlight turns on, shining down on a white-face sad clown, who stands straight, their arms and hands outstretched and face turned upwards. They slowly creep their neck down to face the audience. A small smile graces their red lips, and they begin to sing an excerpt from "Pure Imagination" by Gene Wilder.)

> If you want to view paradise,
> simply look around and view it—
>
> *(They stop singing.)*

I'm looking. Looking through fogged windows at the white blossom trees tangoing with the rain. I'm looking, they don't look back. I draw a heart on the window and the fog covers it instantly. Or maybe it's the trees. They don't want to look.

> *(They start singing.)*
>
> *Anything you want to,*
> *Do it*
>
> *(They stop singing.)*

I want to dance with the trees. I took tango lessons before they sent us all inside. I dance with myself in the mirror with my eyes closed. I open my eyes and see myself, crooked. There's a whistling outside and it's them, the trees and the wind moving with each other, that push and pull my tango instructor crooned about. They're in love… just not with me.

> *Wanna change the world?*
> *There's nothing—*
>
> *(They stop singing. They start again, voice cracking.)*
>
> *Nothing—to it.*

← *"Nothing," by Danielle Levsky. Imagination in quarantine. Sunday May 17, 2020.*

"Our Story Beats, Zay's Story Beats," by Mike Lew and Rehana Lew Mirza. San Diego, CA. May 9, 2020.

← *"Interference Pattern: Quarantine," by Jerry Lieblich. May 19, 2020*

Theater is a
communal ritual.
It is how I feel
connected
How I feel alive
How I feel
belonging
To a greater human
community.

I've felt pretty
numb
Maybe because
We've been denied
that space
That space to feel
together
To grieve
Together

So I want to
create space for us.

We're going to
close our eyes

Drop down into
ourselves

Breathe in

And breathe out

Take a moment to
think of something
or someone
you lost

Bring it close
Don't be afraid
to look it
right in the eye

Think about what
you loved
What you were
gifted
What you hoped
for

The feeling

Whatever this is

Numbness
Anger
Sadness
Frustration

Say yes to it.

It belongs.

It's painful.
It hurts.
I can't take that
away.
But I can see it
And I can hold it
with you.
This is hard
And weird
And new
And none of us
know
how to do this.
I love you,
And it's okay.

This feeling
you are feeling

Where do you feel
it in your body?

Can you locate
that place
Maybe put your
hand on it

And just breathe
into that space?

What does this
space need?

Can you offer
yourself what you
most need?

That's the ritual.

You can open your
eyes.

"Instructions for A Single Audience Member," by Katie Lindsay. Excerpted from a guided walk created for the author's friends, and inspired by Tara Brach. May 12, 2020.

"disCERN/disENTANGLE," by Craig Lucas. The black and white template I colored, wrote and drew upon emanates from the particle accelerator at CERN (the European Organization of Nuclear Research) and charts the first definitive evidence of the previously theorized Higgs boson, the search for which seems to me, in retrospect, quite like our own current collective search for the meaning in this apparent crumbling failure of American democracy to meet any challenges with the effectiveness, respect for science or humility in the face of the common good one would expect the wealthiest nation on earth to bring to bear upon whatever the fuck we want to call this thing that is allowing the Kochs and Betsy Devos to pay people to carry firearms into state legislatures to protest safety measures that will protect their very lives. If we can find the goddam Higgs boson maybe someday we will be able to find the hearts of these people among whom one must of course also include Moscow Mitch McConnell, Gangster Trump, the Dauphin (Kushner) and Fox News' Sans Sannity. Barring that, I am teaching myself to knit for that moment their heads are sliced from their bodies in the public square. Please feel free to bring popcorn and sparklers, confetti, noise makers, MAGA hats. May 9, 2020.

ndow wouldn't remember what I looked at yesterday, or the day before.
ndow wouldn't allow any other conversation but now, now, now.

ndow wouldn't talk about anything but the weather.
ndow wouldn't do anything but talk. It never let the clouds in.
ndow wouldn't repeat the rain.
ndow wouldn't believe what was going on inside.

ndow wouldn't be loyal. It considered itself as belonging as much to the people street as to the owners of the house. It would give a view to either side. It had as oyalty to one-time passersby as the child who had lived with it her whole life.

ndow wouldn't denounce the pervert, the murderer, the peeping tom, the the rock.

ndow wouldn't talk to the door, so jealous.
ndow wouldn't know what to do if someone knocked. It'd probably shatter.
ndow wouldn't let anyone sneak up on us. By the time they knock at the door, dow's been tracking them all the way from the street.

ndow wouldn't stop us from opening a fast food restaurant. People can drive up r lawns. We'll ask them what they want from the bedroom and give them what ant in the kitchen.

ndow wouldn't recognize itself in literature.

ndow wouldn't mind if we opened it every once in a while.
ndow wouldn't mind if we opened ourselves too. Let the window see what we e when the breeze is blowing through us.
ndow wouldn't care if we danced around naked.
ndow wouldn't stop us if cut off all our hair.
ndow wouldn't mind if we turned on all the lights at midnight. Made the window vay mirror. Made ourselves careless about the neighbors watching our dance.

ndow would like to roam around the house.
ndow would like to climb up onto the roof.
ndow would like to cross the street and watch the neighbors for a while.
ndow would like to cross the street and look back over at its home.
ndow would like to travel in a pack, as all the windows move to the wall with the , or to take a look at the best tree. Except the one window. That window 't.

st famous windows are the ones things fall out of: Rapunzel's window, that v in game of thrones.

ndow wouldn't open for the longest time. This was in the house on Edgewood ought it was the story of our marriage. And then one day after a lot of struggle nting and sweat, we succeeded in making it so that the window wouldn't close n I knew it was the story of our divorce.

ndow wouldn't ever commit to being one thing or another; it wouldn't say if it evice for keeping things out of the house: bugs, birds, strangers, rain. Or a device ng things into our lives: breezes, views, smiles, goodbyes.

ndow wouldn't admit its history of violence. In castles they are set so thin so can murder many while never giving up a clear view.

dow wouldn't scowl or smile.
dow wouldn't show the emotion of the house.
dow wouldn't say if the people inside were angry.
dow wouldn't say if the people inside were happy.
dow wouldn't say if the people inside were scared of being found out either

etimes the window would tell us if the people inside were dancing, or running om the bedroom to the laundry room, to grab that forgotten piece of clothing, very least to get the curtains from the drier and stop the windows mouth with ned gag so that it couldn't tell us anything else today.

window was in San Antonio. First floor. Homemade curtains. Single sliding looked out on the alley between our house and the neighbor's garage. It sat e air conditioning. It was the perfect window to sneak out of. To wait for the AC n and then slide it undercover of the shuttering hum and go out and smoke pot beer or walk up and down the street with Connie. Even better are the es of coming back home to that window at 2AM and standing in the dark, for the AC to kick on again to cover the noise I would make coming back in, a ink, a little high, a little happy to be home after being a little gone.

dow wouldn't crack no matter how many bad storms passed by.
dow wouldn't open on any world but the one we'd made.
dow wouldn't locate what we were looking for. We had to find it ourselves by g. If you look away for one second, that's when you missed it.
dow wouldn't be bricked in completely.

dow wouldn't compete with the TV. It only played one channel. One show, 24/7 what is really going on out there."
dow wouldn't compete with the mirror. We could never see ourselves passing

dow wouldn't compete with the refrigerator. We couldn't eat those cats and ose squirrels, those people, no matter how good it looks like they might taste.
dow wouldn't compete with a book. The world is illegible. Undecipherable.
dow wouldn't compete with the windshield. The hungrier you get for change er the window seems to go.
dow wouldn't compete with the internet. The window cannot be distracted. The is one long meditation you can invite yourself into anytime you want.
dow wouldn't compete with other windows. You like that view better? Then ur chair.

dow wouldn't show me my future. Unless my future is two trees. Unless my the weather changing from sunny to rainy and back again? Unless my future is the kids leaving, then you coming home again.

dow wouldn't show me my past. Unless my past is two trees. A green lawn. The bringing less news than I want and more capitalism. Neighbors walking their t my privacy.

dow wouldn't show me the present, only the surface of the present. I never hy you came home.

dow wouldn't bring back my brother.

dow would bring back my brother.
dow would let me see him walking down the sidewalk.
dow would let me imagine that the sidewalk was buckling underneath him.
dow would give me time to think: do I let the ghost in this time? Do I forgive time? Do I act like nothing happened again?
dow would then laugh and laugh and laugh. That wasn't my brother. That was ner stranger wearing the same outline, the same haircut for a hat, going ere else.

dow would trick the birds. Invite them into the house and then BANG! The would slam shut and we'd hear the panes laughing. We'd hear the window "did you see how stupid that bird was?"

dow wouldn't tell us what happened at night.
dow wouldn't tell us what happened while we were away at work.

The window wouldn't ever lie to us. It wouldn't let us believe it was sunny outside when it wasn't. Wouldn't let us believe our guests weren't late when they were. Wouldn't let us believe the car hadn't been broken into. We could hear the alarm, we could see our empty driveway, feel the rain beating on the roof.

The window wouldn't count for us, or keep track of our departures, or be held accountable in any way. I will want to know how many times I have left and how many times I have come home. I will want to know how many times my children have left and how many times they have come home. I will want my children's number to be one more leaving than returning. I will want my number to be one less.

The window wouldn't mourn. You can cover it with a heavy black drape, but we all know there is a space between the pane and the cloth of the curtain that is bright as day.

The window wouldn't stop vomiting my clothes onto the lawn. The house was sick of me.

The window wouldn't show us the civil war.
The window wouldn't let me jump.
The window wouldn't let me fall.
The window wouldn't let my spirit push my body over the cliff of my life.

The window wouldn't starve the air of motes.

The window wouldn't let us take off our clothes until the sun went down.
The window wouldn't judge us for smoking dope in the middle of the day.
The window wouldn't cover our nakedness.
The window wouldn't censor us. It showed us as we were to the neighborhood.

The window wouldn't select better curtains. We dressed it once a decade and it never complained.

The window wouldn't deny it was the child of the door.
The window would shudder when the door slammed.
The window would announce new arrivals.
The window would stay awake all night making sure the family was locked up safe.

The window wouldn't spend any time on the corner of the house. The window is a flat creature.

The window wouldn't fight the ivy, nature's blinds, slowly closing from the ground up.

I remember a few windows in New York. I remember one especially, above the bed where Lana and I slept. Where I slept and Lana kept watch, like a little Kilroy, peeping over the edge to look down on Brooklyn down below. We lived on the 300 block of South Bedford Avenue. There was a needle exchange down below and a crack deli across the street. Lana would stay up all night watching people come and go. The business day starting at night. I remember one night waking up to a loud pop and Lana telling me that Eddie the fencer had just been shot.

I remember a window in Paris that opened out into an alley.

The window wouldn't promote a fantasy: everything is made of glass: the trees, the walls of the house, people—everything is perfectly see-thru and then only our windows would be wood or stone... little panes of solidity we could look at when we wanted to block the clear nothingness all around us.

The window wouldn't admit that the future would change it. Glass would go out of fashion. We would have an era of new plastics, followed by an era of magnetic fields. We lived in the era of glass and it had not really been all that long, as far as eras go.

Windows of fire in a house of stone.
Windows of tears in the house of a face.
Windows of words in a house of silence.

The window wouldn't relax. Always stiff. Always standing up right. Always watching

The window wouldn't stop watching me while I slept. It's one eye looked at my bed. It couldn't stop showing me off to the moon.

The window wouldn't break up with you, even after I did. It kept looking for you coming down the street. It kept hoping you would throw a little gravel at its pane. Wake it up in the middle of the night. Put your hands on its frame again and lift up like a mother lifting her daughter into the air.

The window wouldn't admit how many criminals had looked through its glass.

The window wouldn't stop talking to the trees and the grass outside. It kept telling them about furniture and floors. It gave the sunbeam a slow tour of the living room.

The window wouldn't admit that cheese was its closest relatives. A swiss cousin, full of holes and of course that makes you and I its mice.

I remember a window in college, one pane of which was broken, covered in cardboard and taped up, like a bandage on a view. And at a party a woman sat next to this window all night, drawing on the cardboard in pencil, and as the morning came up, I could see that she had got it right, she had drawn the view exactly as it would have been, minus the drunks on the lawn and the trash of cups.

The window wouldn't stop telling all our bright secrets.
The window wouldn't stop calling out to the curious passersby.
The window wouldn't stop coughing light out into the neighborhooded night.
The window wouldn't stop leaking our party into the neighbor's jealous minds.

The window wouldn't be patient with rest of the house. The window thought everything that happened should happen within its view.

The window wouldn't tell us who it liked to look at most. But it was probably the cat.
The window wouldn't confess. But it had seen everything.

The window wouldn't open onto the past.
The window wouldn't let me see you again.
The window wouldn't give me another look at Halloween 2011, we sitting around the apartment and suddenly decided to do a speed challenge and get into costume in five minutes. We ran around grabbing clothes we hadn't worn in years. You put a scarf around your hair and I drew an eye patch on my face with eye liner. You put on a long skirt and I put on a three-piece suit. We a medium and a river boat gambler. We never left the house. We didn't trick or treat or go to a party. We were our own fun. And the window wouldn't show us off to anyone.

The window wouldn't bulge out with the pressure of the world.
The window wouldn't buckle with the weight of the snow on the roof.

The window wouldn't preference humans over the rest of the animal kingdom. It was just as happy for the cats to look out it, for the dog to lie in the sunlight, for the flies to climb across it looking for a way in.

The window wouldn't let the curtains keep it covered forever. Like a long dress with a slit in it, the light pours out of the secret places.

The window wouldn't let the day wake us for the longest time. The window tried to hold the light back. The window slowed down the sun. The window wanted us to keep dreaming of a time when cool breezes and long nights were our treasure.

The window wouldn't change the channel.
The window wouldn't shine in black and white.
The window wouldn't let us adjust the contrast.
The window wouldn't focus on the strangers.

← *"The Window Would/The Window Wouldn't," by Kirk Lynn. Every morning I stare out my window and write about it, on going until I have 100,000 pages. May 13, 2020.*

At first there was the giddiness of a snow day, when our spring break was extended. I welcomed the pause and rejoiced at the quiet roads and the photographs of clean air. But reality set in with the death of actor Mark Blum; terrifying and tragic things were happening. It's like we were all having the same bad dream--with its dream logic. We had to stay inside because something invisible but dangerous is out there.

A *New Yorker* cartoon listed the days of the week with the first half of each name crossed out, leaving only a list of seven "days." Back when we worried about catching the flu, a friend had recommended that I take a daily probiotic and each pill is helpfully marked with a different day of the week. But my days feel too short, despite the lengthening daylight. I walk the dog, grade a single student play, answer a few emails, and it's time for the evening glass of wine, when we turn towards Netflix, as plants turn towards the sun.

I'm now obsessed by the naming of birds and wildflowers, returning to the pleasures of an agrarian life, except that I have Plant Snap and iNaturalist. Walking through the woods with the dog, I should be thinking deep thoughts but instead I find myself wondering…*whatever happened to that electric massager thing?* I've been taking stock of what I own, literally, wondering whether old leather eyeglass cases and a broken antique barometer can be fixed.

My pants are growing tight, despite my virtual exercise. For Zumba, I roll up the rug in my bedroom. For online yoga classes, I put it down. While living in Ohio, I've been able to study with two excellent LA yoga teachers—one of the few pandemic wins. Someone on Facebook, joking about gaining weight, referred to her Covid-19, then scrambled to assure everybody that she wasn't sick.

An ad from Facebook recommended Manduka yoga supplies and I paid a premium for their "professional" mat—which was money well-spent. Packages are thrilling, magazines are lifelines. But all the articles seem to fall into three categories—how did this happen, here's how it happened, and what do we do now?

When lying on my new yoga mat, I can see the dust balls gathering under the bed and the dust in the claw feet of the antique dresser. I've channeled my anxiety into cleaning since I'm now home to see the dirt. I tidy my grown sons' bedrooms without knowing when I will see them again. I've also started going through tubs of old correspondence. Some names ring distant bells but if I can't put a face to them, the letters go in the trash.

In CURSE OF THE STARVING CLASS the father expresses his love by doing the family's laundry; my father used to polish our shoes. When the lockdown was about to begin, I reached for the laundry detergent instead of the toilet paper. After washing and collecting bags full of spurned clothing, I discovered there was no place to donate them. Goodwill was closed and their outdoor bins were spilling over. Either there were no workers to collect it or nobody wanted to touch used clothing. Will there still *be* thrift stores when all this is over?

The September premiere of my new play was canceled, with the "hope" of doing it in 2021. I try to believe that everything happens for a reason, that the delay might prove beneficial somehow. My parents were unable to have children during the first several years of their marriage, which proved to be a fortuitous delay when their children were born *after* they'd found a polio vaccine.

My rage at Trump grows exponentially, because in addition to killing people, his negligence has managed to wound, or possibly kill, the two industries that sustain me—higher education and the theater. In a recent *Atlantic* essay Caitlin Flanagan wrote that anger is often a cover for sorrow, but in this case I'm not so sure.

Still there are waves of happiness, when I realize I don't have to be anywhere or see anyone. I've come to realize how I was perpetually *rushing*. Life under lockdown is not that different from a writer's usual life. And while we've had to give things up, I still have so much—a salary, food, companionship, a comfortable house, and the hope of an imminent regime change.

"Sheltering in Place," by Wendy MacLeod.
May 15, 2020.

I dont want to be in anymore...

But being out fills me with

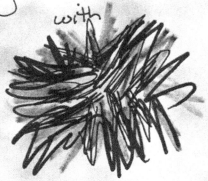

who knows what is beyond the door

"Contemplations before grabbing my keys, latex gloves, hand sanitizer and mask," by Jennifer Maisel. Not ready to face the day. May 9, 2020.

ZOOM READINGS ARE THE FAST FOOD OF THEATRE-MAKING.

KINDA GROSS AND NOT VERY NOURISHING, BUT DEF BETTER THAN STARVING TO DEATH.

← *"Better Than Starving," by Chelsea Marcantel. Conceived after the realizing that an artist can NEED something and also DISLIKE it. May 15, 2020.*

I have new scars where there were none. I couldn't stand carrying around two large breasts everywhere I went. A stitch sticks out of the new incision and pricks me. Strange scabs, bruises pink, yellow, purple, brownish, iridescent.

When the doctor opened my paper gown she said, "Oh yes, you're a perfect candidate." I was afraid I this surgery was tempting fate: I could be smote by a god I didn't believe in and die on the table.

Today it's raining sideways, on an angle, maybe 40 degrees. It could be 30. I am not supposed to pull the stitches out before their time. I want their time to be now. Pricky threads.

The year I was 15, I slept with a black and white poster of Marilyn Monroe on the ceiling over my bed, another Marilyn above my headboard, and a sepia-toned James Dean as Jett Rink. When I read that Marilyn slept in her bra, I did too. Underwire. That sounds ludicrous to me now.

The doctor says, "Everyone has asymmetrical breasts." She measures my areola to armpit, the top of my breasts to the areola, and underneath. She pronounces it *or-reel*. I panic: how many times in life I've mispronounced areola. Then I panic that she's wrong and is maybe a bad doctor? She reads out my measurements. My breasts are symmetrical, but she doesn't comment. She says, "You will be so happy after surgery." I want to ask her about *or-reel*. I never do.

Now I have new tits. She moved my or-reels to match the size of my new old tits. Or old new tits? My nipples look the same. My or-reels look as if they're wearing lip liner. The incisions are an angry pink with long yellowed bruises.

It was good to work today. Yesterday I was in a weird funk--not weird--but Friday night I hit the time for tears. First time I cried during this Covid thing. All the loved ones who lose each other. I took for granted the privilege to hold someone's hand, as their body is vaguely present, lessening, waiting for the cold to stiffen them. To kiss their forehead. One last time. Those are the laws of illness, in the time before now.

My tits hurt like little war engines. These incisions are called anchors but they look more like upside-down smiling T's. Beneath the incisions are stitches with little knots. They will dissolve one day, but they are trying to poke their way out of me. Imagine ten toothpicks *inside* your breast and poking out? I can't take it and I act drastically: With tweezers I go in to grab the thin thread-like fishing line. Am I the bait? An hour later, I pull one knot out enough to snip it with kitchen scissors. I am a WWI medic! My doctor prescribes a topical antibiotic and 40 pills as a precaution.

I'm glad I live in a world in which I have access to antibiotics.

It occurs to me that being quarantined is what it felt like to be one of the Brontë sisters, small-town life in the 1800's, a day's carriage ride away for any visitors. The excitement of the arrival of a new face! That was your one tinder.

Once I had a girlfriend for a very short time, a shrink who once worked on a psych ward. She said she'd had to physically subdue patients. I asked her to try to hold me down. No woman ever could hold me down, I wanted someone to contain me as I wilded out, taming me. She did, and I felt held and spent. She turned out to be a total asshole narcissist; as quickly as I thought we'd fallen for each other, she'd actually just used me to get back at her ex. Her ex, however great she may have been, looked like a troll doll.

Reader, are you out there?

I wonder if it matters. Does it? The date is Thursday, May 7, 2020.

"New old tits. Old new tits," by Winter Miller.
From 4/something/20 - 5/something20.

EVELYN
I confused the oven with the dryer.

AMIR
How?

EVELYN
I sleepwalk. Done some odd things in the past. According to Christopher, he once found me, at 3 in the morning, trying to install wall-to-wall carpeting on the driveway. When did I start? And where did I get the carpet? And you know what? I had exactly enough. But this time, I wasn't asleep! I was wide-awake, pushing the guest duvet into the oven. Then, I turned it to 450 degrees and even set a timer for 10 minutes.

AMIR
Was there a turkey in the dryer?

EVELYN
No, thank goodness. Only a few cold cuts and a can of Diet Pepsi.

AMIR
Jesus.

EVELYN
I feel like I'm falling apart! The madness is taking over and even even even my words are getting weird. I'm missing up every-time I'm splaying! It combs out in gobbity-glook – NO! My tight hand just Phil off!

AMIR
Evelyn! Evelyn I'm coming over – rules be damned!

EVELYN
Oh n
    o!
        H
      e   m
       l p   e

← *"Disintegration," by Michael Mitnick. The World. May 11, 2020.*

Good Evening folks!
> *When we gather again, will we do so in the evenings?*
> *Will outdoor performance venues be the first to reopen, the safest?*
> *Should we say "Good Morning"?*
> *Or "Good Afternoon"?*
> *Maybe it's best to simply say "Welcome."*

Thank you so much for being here.
> *Here in this particular place?*
> *Here at this particular time?*
> *Here where I can hear you*
> *without any mediator or interference?*
> *Here when physical proximity is a gift and not a threat?*

We're so glad that you've joined us.
> *We're so glad you survived.*
> *We're so glad we survived.*

…
…
…

> *Our stories will be different now.*
> *The way we tell them*
> *The way we make them*
> *The way we share them will be different now.*
> *And the people who hunger for them will be different too.*

This performance will not include an intermission.
> *The intermission we've taken was long enough.*

Please be sure to turn your cell phones off.
> *Can you even imagine?*
> *Shared space. Disconnected screens.*
> *Shared breath. Synced heartbeats.*

And now, without any further ado, I invite you to lean forward and enjoy...*this play*
> *There will be plays*
> *And playing*
> *Together*
> *Someday*

"A Coronavirus Curtain Speech," by Anne G. Morgan. Meditating on a mundane task. May 14, 2020.

ACT 1

SCENE 1

(An apartment building on West 97th Street near Riverside Drive. RACHEL EPSTEIN, very pregnant, is attempting to pack. She talks to her husband who's offstage.)

RACHEL
I don't know where things are supposed to go. How do you categorize tchotchkes? Well, you could say I just categorized them: tchotchkes. But we've got so many different kinds of tchotchkes. And should we pack cleaners? I don't want to touch the toilet bowl cleaner because what if it touches other things and then they're contaminated and we don't remember and then the baby is going to put them in her mouth. Everyone is giving me things for a girl now. I don't think we should've told anyone. I'm happy we found out. But we should've kept it a secret.

(AARON WILCOMBE, her husband, enters. He's dressed in a button down flannel and sweats. He takes off headphones.)

AARON
I'm sorry, were you talking? I was listening to a podcast called How To Fix America.

RACHEL
How do you fix it?

AARON
Communication.

RACHEL
That sounds facile.

AARON
I mean it's more complicated than that. But the point is we have a lot in common.

RACHEL
How about if people stop being racist, sexist, unloving pigs? How about that?

AARON
That would help too.

← *"Boulevard Comedy," by Matt Moses. May 11, 2020.*

- buy toilet paper
- send wedding invitations
- call Mom and Dad
- buy beans
- cancel March
- repot plants
- get wedding dress altered
- download "Zoom"
- read some books
- check in with artist friends - are they okay?
- get takeout from every neighborhood restaurant
- set hours for working from home
- try new recipes - maybe with beans
- order masks
- don't have a panic attack
- keep the plants alive
- cancel April
- decide if we should postpone the wedding
- research how to produce Zoom events
- cancel transit pass
- update directing portfolio
- stick to the hours I set for working from home
- start meditating
- cancel May
- send Mother's Day card
- masks have not arrived - make masks out of old t-shirts instead
- cancel wedding venue
- call wedding caterer
- hug partner
- read only happy books
- should I get a bike?
- prep for new play workshop on Zoom
- decide if I should apply to grad school
- write letter to childhood friend
- did I water the plants???
- try yoga
- cancel June?
- make some art
- buy Father's Day card
- take a deep breath

← *"To Do," by Allie Moss. Compiled from tasks that I've crossed off in my bullet journal. May 15, 2020.*

ESSAY #5

used to be
then it was

a field
a massive net

the process was conducted
on its feet

something can be done with that
most things some things can be done with
they could be made
provided there's interest
and probably could be
though perhaps without the (or use a euphemism)

just perhaps things

it's interesting, it isn't finished and when I get home
I will need to smash it

THEN I HAD A DREAM I WAS A TRAIN A LOCOMOTIVE SPEWING SMOKE OUT OF MY SMOKESTACK AND IT FELT GOOD TO LET THAT SMOKE OUT I WAS THE FASTEST TRAIN POLISHED STEEL I WAS GOD'S TRAIN I COULD GO ANYWHERE TRACKS APPEARED BEFORE ME OFF I GO CHOOCHOO

IS A BUG
IS A DINOSAUR
IS A GHOST
HAS A MOTH'S BODY
IS A GRIFFIN
LIVES IN A TREE
HAS ELF EARS
LEVITATES
IS UPSIDE DOWN
COVERED IN SCALES
IS OMNISCENT

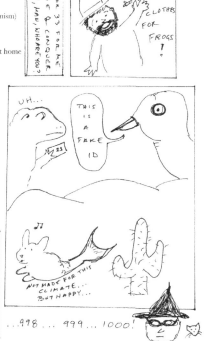

"lunchbox papers (essay #5)," by Gregory S. Moss. Number 5 in a series of 100 essays. Equinox, March 19, 2020.

2019

2020

- LosT my father.
- Left LA.
- Fell IN LoVe with NYC again.
- Lived with Grief.

?? But...
I hAVe HOPE.

ANYA Mama! . . . Mama, you're crying? Dear, kind, good Mama, my own, my beautiful, I love you . . . I bless you. The cherry orchard's sold, it's gone now, that's true, true, true, but don't cry, Mama, you've still got your life ahead of you, you've still got your good, pure heart . . . Come with me, come, dearest, let's go away from here, let's go! . . . We'll plant a new orchard, more splendid than this one, you'll see it, you'll understand, and joy, peaceful, profound joy will sink into your heart, like the sun when night falls, and you'll smile, Mama! Let's go, dearest! Let's go! . . .

CURTAIN

← *"Hopeful Grief," by Rebecca Mozo, contemplating the art of moving forward, while still honoring the losses. May 21, 2020.*

ZANDELEM

How scared am I? Now is the moment Mum says, "Why tell me, eh?! Gather the tribe, find Chief, say, "I am a child of sunlight. Under moon, stars, between earth are my Ancestors. Oh!, I fuck gay." Then see what becomes of your life." Next thing Mum says in her mosquito voice. It's true, it stings malaria when she says, "Out. NOW!" I swallow rejection. Spoonfuls. Then go. Step after step leaving when longing while loving her. Becoming less me; becoming more me; becoming another me; becoming unknown to me. I'm scared like that. The pathway from me to any future is desire drowning laced with courage. When I do look back, over this kah-shoulder right here, I see a woman who is no longer my Mum. Still perfect, still beautiful, still bathed in sunlight yet —she's just as invisible as I am. Next step. My heart sings BOOM kara kara BOOM. Will I live homeless? Abandoned? Nothingness? Raped? Invisible? Erased? Unaccepted? Unlovable? Abused? Futureless? On the wrong side of darkness forever? Is that who I am? Fearful whenever fearless? But I say it proudly: "I am African". More proudly: "I fuck gay."

Oh yes. I say it because if I don't, I will live my life in fear. With a PhD in Shame. I say it because—as a Black queer, my purpose moves me through everything created to kill me. That is my medicine. Faith in my Queer Ancestors. Who transform pain into purpose, purpose into a better world. Because somewhere, somehow, as I look to an unknown future, I see you. Clearly. Certain in my uncertainity.

"Homeless In the AfterLife," by Nick Hadikwa Mwaluko. May 14, 2020.

1

*A projection across the back wall of the stage reads **MONDAY**.*

KATIE, 30s, tired but cheerful, sits at her laptop. She's excited. She has waited all day for a little time to write. She takes a luxurious sip of coffee. Opens a new doc. Suddenly, from offstage—

> A TODDLER'S VOICE
> Mama!!!! Mamaaaaaaaaa!

> KATIE
> You ok, bud? I'm coming!

She leaves. END SCENE.

2

*A projection across the back wall of the stage reads **TUESDAY**.*

Katie sits at her laptop. She's excited. She has waited all day for—

> A TODDLER'S VOICE
> Mama! I'm an excavator, and I'm stuck! Rescue meeeee!

She laughs, and leaves. END SCENE.

3

*A projection across the back wall of the stage reads **WEDNESDAY**.*

Katie sits at— We hear a CRASH offstage. She LOOKS. END SCENE.

4

*A projection across the back wall of the stage reads **THURSDAY**.*

No Katie. The laptop sits open. We wait. Nope. END SCENE.

5

*A projection across the back wall of the stage reads **FRIDAY**.*

Katie sits at her laptop. She's excited. She has waited all day for a little time to write. She reaches for— She LEAVES. Returns with coffee. Nice. Checks the time. Excellent. Listens… Silence. She starts to type. Stops. Grabs her phone. Scrolls News. Frowns. Puts it down. Grabs it again.

> KATIE
> Toilet paper… felt and pipe cleaners… Markers…

She one-click orders. Puts the phone down. Lifts her hands to the keys—

> A TODDLER'S VOICE
> Ma—!

Lights out. END PLAY.

"Priorities," by Katie Locke O'Brien. on the occasion of her brain becoming sour cream. May 14, 2020.

"Dream of a Nervous Man," by Kira Obolensky. A short flat play inspired by Kafka. May 14, 2020.

← *"Virus Writing," by Laurel Ollstein. What came out instead of my play. May 12, 2020.*

"but now this," by Matthew Paul Olmos & April Dawn Guthrie. Created 7–9 months into their relationship. May 13, 2020.

Everyone has things to say.
I know they do.
And I listen.
Like a lot. I do.
And I read everything.
I try to anyway.
I read it.
I take it in.
And I am exercising and doing the yoga and holding it all in and together and along with everything and everyone and I am cooking.
A lot.
And I am planting some seeds and things and clearing brush and leaves and dead branches and thinking about compost and how to use the compost.
Delighted by a garter snake and an oriole.
The oriole is beautiful.
It is.

And

There is nothing to do about it.

"Actions," by Kristen Palmer. Written on Mother's Day. May 10, 2020.

DARIA: We were sitting at socially distanced tables at a diner on the west side. She was reading The Master and Margarita by Mikhail Bulgakov. I was getting my PhD in Slavic languages with a track in Russian lit. I mean. What are the odds? I'm going to say this and you're going to have to trust me when I say it, okay? Trust me and don't think I'm a jerk. I've [M. Reacts] had a hard life. There was a car accident. Followed by a motorcycle accident. What can I say? The accidents messed up my spine. And during the pandemic, I felt, for the fist time, *everyone* knows what being ill or the fear of becoming ill, is like. Before the virus, if you were sick or chronically ill, you dealt with it, quietly, without a fuss. People don't need to hear about that shit. Unless you have cancer. Cancer is okay. I mean cancer *sucks*, but if you have it, you can be out loud about it, find support. Everyone's touched by cancer. You're a hero for surviving it. For having it. Now literally everyone could get ill, and you couldn't see it, and it wasn't your fault if you got it, and it could be deadly. And you could be in a lot of pain. I thought, this could be a game changer. Right? Like, if everyone has to worry about their health, all the time, the way sick people do, then, maybe America, the world, becomes a kinder, gentler place. Maybe our work environments become more forgiving. Maybe our health care system becomes more equitable. Virginia Woolf wondered why poets and writers didn't write about illness the way they do about love and war. How do we include the last excluded group – the ill, the disabled, is what I was wondering, that day, when I met Miriam, at the diner, after restrictions in our city had loosened. I wanted to touch her hair. I

[Don't hide]

*"two misfits fall in love & change the world
(or at least how they see it)," by Lina Patel.
A near future duologue for two women
about love and illness. Begun May 4, 2020.*

i woke up today
unable to remember
this is just the second act
and wouldn't you like to know
what happens next?

← *"the protagonist at wits end," by Christopher O. Peña. May 11, 2020.*

This isn't my plant, but this is my favorite plant out of all of the plants that aren't mine. I don't know its name. This plant eats the sunshine like it owned it, and wiggles in the air like it was made of it, and I can see it stretch, and burrow, and crisp, and fade in tiny, mysterious dots on the leaves, and strange little brown curlings on the stem, and when its leaves are new they are thin and shiny and face the sun and react to everything: a spritz, a pat, a cloudy day— and when they are old they see nothing and never seem to notice my spritzes, and pats, and cloudy days, and I don't want to be like that— I think— though it seems nice somedays— I think that's not why I like this plant –that's not why— that sucks and that's boring—and some young people are just stupid and not just in Florida—and some old people are still soft and don't shut down just because their skin thickens. I'm sorry. I'm not judging the plant—or anyone else—but especially not the plant for having soft, young leaves and hard, old leaves. That's insane. I'm not— it's not even my plant—who am I to judge it? Mandy trusted me. She trusted me to take care of her plants so that we could stay here, and to be honest, when she said we could stay at her place while Alec— the other roommate— we've never met— was stuck in NY and she was staying at her boyfriend's parents' mansion in the hills I thought she was joking. Not about the mansion— I knew that his parents had a mansion— though I do have questions about it—but about the plants. Mattering. Or not mattering, but, I guess, like— thinking of plants as actual THINGS that need care and attention like a kid, or an old person would — I just. Yeah. I didn't. Think of them that way. Before. But I was grateful for anywhere to stay that had enough space for two, so we're here now. My girlfriend doesn't take care of the plants. I point out new leaves to her and she remarks in wonder—but I know that she'd rather sit at the window and watch the neighbors take their dogs on walks up and down the street every day. I prefer it inside with the plants. And not cause it's calm or, like, some stupid home catalog spread, but cus they are fighting, and trying not to outgrow their pots, and reacting poorly to bad days, too. This is my favorite plant out of all the plants that aren't mine. I don't know its name. I called it Roberta for a while. Then Shaw. Then Kissy. Then Gorf. Then Windslit. Then Chad. But I knew that all those names were wrong, of course they were. Last night I couldn't take it any longer. I snuck out of bed and crawled to the plant— wiggling, shriveling, buckling inside my own skin despite the fact that I don't drink anymore— I crawled out of bed— careful not to wake my girlfriend—skin clammy with thirst and sweat— I pulled myself on hands and knees down the hall, and into the dark living room to ask the plant its name. In the dark living room I could almost hear the plants breathing around me. Please, I whispered— I know you aren't mine—but I can't keep loving you, and watching you, and feeding you and not know who you are. Please tell me that I can call you. I lay on the floor beside the plant to show it that I was serious about my servitude. On the cold floor the plant seemed to loom above me, as though taken aback by my forward question. Please, I

won't tell anyone—I swore. Outside a siren squealed, and a car alarm sang, and a neighbor screamed in Russian at his wife— but the plant said nothing. I raised my fingers gently up its spine, said a prayer to the wilting leaves, leaned close and whispered to the dirt: help. Suddenly the leaves swayed, the roots stirred—dirt on dirt— air in air— leaves to palm— stem to eye—rip—stretch— shoot—the plant stepped out of its pot like someone who hadn't moved in a long, long, long, long time. Silhouetted in the moonlight, the plant towered over me—no longer mine to care for, but mine to fear. It leaned close—closer—closer—closer—eyelash to leaf— teeth to root—how easy it is to snap a bone when you think about it—closer—closer— you can't call 911 if you aren't a "you" anymore— closer—closer—what will my girlfriend think when she finds me here—alone— sweating—overtaken by dead earth—laying on the ground beside an empty pot—closer—closer— maybe the plant will take my name—maybe it has no name and it needs mine—maybe Mandy knew what she was doing when she brought us here—maybe she knew this was the only way for her plant to—suddenly the plant kneeled down at my feet, whispered its name into the hole on the bottom of my sock, and sat back down in its tiny ceramic kingdom. There has never been a name so perfect in all the world as the name that the plant whispered into the hole in the bottom of my sock last night. But I'm no fucking snitch, so you can get bent if you think I'm telling. But I will tell you: this is my favorite plant—not because it is mine— but because I am its.

"I AM ITS" by Roxie Perkins. Written at 5 AM while still awake at 5 AM. May 10th, 2020.

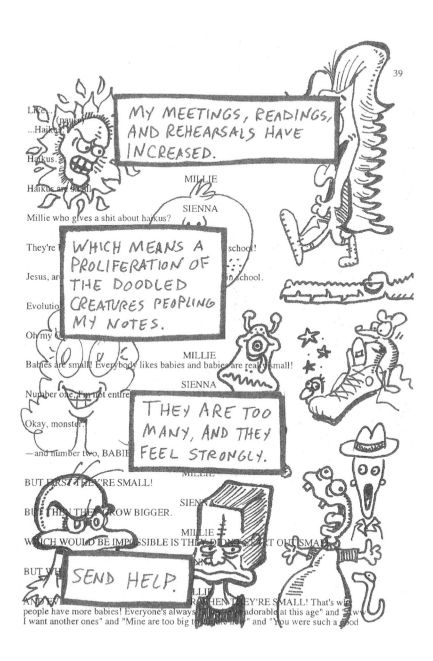

"Invasive Species," by Eric Pfeffinger. Created instead of going to another Zoom thing. May 17, 2020.

6:45pm. Bedtime routine. The boys take a bath, Andrew nurses a little, we read books. Lights off. I sing "Moon River" twice. 7:30pm. Bedtime. *Goodnight, Andrew. Now you're going to go to sleep by yourself. I know it's going to be a little different, but you can do it and Mommy and Daddy will be right outside the door. We love you!* 7:31pm. We turn on a movie for Sam and wait for the crying to start. 7:41pm. The crying starts. I set a timer for five minutes. 7:46pm. First check-in. *Hi sweetheart, it's Mommy, I know this is really hard, but you're doing such a great job, and I'm so proud of you. Please try to go to sleep and I'll come check on you soon.* I set a timer for ten minutes. Sam wants to know whether it's possible that he got "the coronavirus" at the urgent care when he had an ear infection two days ago. 7:57pm. Second check-in. *Hi Andrew, it's Mommy, I love you so much, and I know you can do it. I'll be back in a little while.* Sam is eating popcorn mixed with candy, he's hyper and over-tired and can't stop biting his nails. I wonder if any good child psychologists are working with kids over Zoom. They must be. I set a timer for fifteen minutes. 8:43pm. Third check-in. 9:05pm. Fourth check-in. Shit, Sam is going to have to sleep in our room tonight if this keeps going. The book says most babies fall asleep within an hour. Maybe we shouldn't have taken him out of the SNOO cold turkey. 9:20pm. Fifth check-in. It's been almost two hours since bedtime. Is it possible Andrew will just… never fall asleep? Google "baby awake all night sleep training". Sam goes to bed in our room. He cries. *This is not how I thought sharing a room with my brother would be. This is not how it was supposed to be.* 9:34pm. Andrew is asleep. 10:42pm. Andrew is awake. 10:59pm. Andrew starts to cry. I start to cry. 11:04pm. First check-in. *Hi Andrew, it's Mommy. It's not time to eat yet. Please go back to sleep now. I love you.* 11:10pm. Andrew is asleep. 11:21pm. Breastfeed for 20 minutes. I have to remember to call tomorrow to defer Amex payments for another month. Hopefully I can get through to a person this time. 2:00am. Breastfeed 14 minutes. We're going to run out of fruit in a couple of days, I should order a produce box. 4:30am. Breastfeed 10 minutes. God this new rocking chair is comfortable. I almost fall asleep. But I don't fall asleep. 5:40am. Andrew is awake. 5:46am. Andrew is crying. 5:51am. First check-in. *Andrew, it's not time to get up yet, my love. Please go back to sleep and I'll see you in a little while.* Sam wants to know what's going on. I rub his head and stare at the ceiling. He falls asleep, kicking me in the stomach. 6:02am. Andrew is asleep. 6:36am. Andrew wakes up for the day. *Good morning buddy! I'm so proud of you! You did it! Are you proud of yourself? That was so hard but you did it!* 6:45am. I drink 4 cups of coffee in 15 minutes. I scan the baby's face to see if he holds a grudge. 7:00am. Sam has a temper tantrum because he doesn't want his ear drops this morning. I enter last night's sleep data into my tracker. Still two hours to go until nap.

"Controlled Crying," by Rebecca Phillips Epstein. Sleep training log for Andrew (5 months), on night 54 of isolation. May 9, 2020.

There

is

nothing

left...

except

Everything.

*"I Don't Know Anymore," by Daria Polatin.
An exercise in truth. May 9, 2020.*

ME: The day my brain turned inside out was the same day the theaters closed. I had a ticket to a brand new musical and decided to donate the amount before the announcement stormed the Internet. At that point, my brain still sloshed upright in my skull and made logical choices. It said:

BRAIN: Hello! It's just a show. Stay home. There will be more shows.

ME: But then I shook my head and shook my head harder until the contents of my brain spread over my scalp like an inside-out Halloween sweater—

BRAIN: I know. I know. It's more than a show.

ME: Yes. It's so much more than a show.

"Postcard from the Inside of My Brain," by Christina Quintana (CQ). A tribute to my addled mind in quarantine. May 10, 2020.

An oak titmouse perches above the little garden at the house where we are quarantining in California. The titmouse, Fiddleneck Titmouse, claims to be an archeologist and a hobbyist impressionist painter. My girlfriend digs up shards of pottery. Fiddleneck scolds me for not helping. How tactfully he excavates, how easily he puts together his nest. How well-thought out his life has been.

Until last year, I worked in two worlds: New York City and a farm in the Hudson Valley.

March is the time to start seedlings;
The brandywine, the rose, the prudence purple
The sungold.

April is the time for preparing beds of earth,
Time for planting onions;
The redwing, the walla walla,
and the rosso di tropea,
the Venus di Milo of aliums.

May is for the sowing of flowers;
The dianthus, the petunias, the poppy,
and the bergamot,
Sweet relish of bees.

In June old friends come back to visit:
the anise hyssop, the rose, the mulberry and walnut,
and even the cucumber beetle,
O, honorable enemy.

Now, there's no job. Now, all the jobs are gone. I've more grey in my hair.

I look back over the shards of Knossos while Fiddleneck Titmouse watches, stuffed into a tweed jacket. He has a rather big bottom and wears a ridiculous grey crest on his head.

The farmer taught me to cook for other people and keep the doors unlocked for company. He taught me that this was the most important thing. Dinners at the farm were chaotic affairs; greasy piles of meat, fresh greens, steep pots of boiled new potatoes and dill, three loaves of bread, fresh cream, mason jars of rye and whiskey, stained with the hard calcium of well water. Pull up a chair, we'd say. Everybody did. Friends, neighbors, artists, babies, cats, dogs. We were cash poor but rich in hot tables of plenty.

Now I try to explain to the folks back home.
How I could never earn more than minimum wage.
Now I spend a lot of time alone. Except for the titmouse.

It's easy to say: Follow your heart and things will end up okay.
It's not as simple as that.
You'll end up in a muddle.
The heart is incapable.

"Knossos," by Stella Fawn Ragsdale. May 15, 2020, in California.

Clap along? 5-6-7-8-

lilbit broke
& a lilbit broken
stay way from me Come closer come close
defrost cherries in the microwave oven
stay way from me come close

                        cat get settled on lap that's mine--
                        ---[stay way from me come closer
                        come close]--
                        i mean I think this lap's still mine
                        [stay way away Come close]
                        bodies don't work in this fuckeduptime
                        [stay way from me come close come
                        close]
                        --catbody or mine?--
                        --Whoops There goes the line--
                        [stay way from me come close]

time don't work in this fuckeduptime
[stay way from me come close Come close]
wine still works Most of the time
[stay way from me come close]

watch stupid NOVA bout   black black holes
don't talk to me about   black black holes
think you know bout   black black holes
i'm who knows bout   black black holes

start as a cavity   in my   mouth
got no dentist   drill it out
   space-time   thicks up   weeks go by
  [stare that   webcam   right in the eye]
cavity grow   out past my face
widening rag- hole   time and space
grow to a gravity gobbling horror
laugh track Netflix scratch at the door
sucks you in like a darkening star
far is near
near is far
funny is sad
blessed is broken
sleep til noon
endless zoom
stay way from me Stay way from me Stay way from me Stay way from me
stay way from me   [come close]

"blackhole comeclose," by Molly Rice. May 14, 2020.

I want someone to cover my body in that exfoliator thing and rub it in and then pour a bucket of warm water across me
I want so many people to hug me
I want my mom to hold me
I want my mom to hold me
I want my mom to hold me
I want to touch my mom's face
I want my mom to hold my face in her hands
I want to feel the veins on my mom's hands, the way they puff out
I want a yoga instructor to push my shoulders down
I want a masseuse to massage my back
I want to run so hard my legs feel sore in that nice way
I want to feel warm in the sun and fall asleep like that
I want to hug a little kid
I want to be in a sensory deprivation room

dark

pitch black

quiet

"How do you want to be touched," by Anya Richkind. A writing exercise. May 11, 2020.

(lights up)

(pause)

(pause)

← *"250 Little Ghost Lights, All Turned On," by Colette Robert. Created 64 Days after My Last Day in a Physical Theater. May 15, 2020.*

The body is an archive of trauma
Scripts lodged in our nervous system
Triggers don't know stories in the body
Narrative Patterns of consciou~~s~~ + unconscious

to experience that pain, but I feel
somewhat cured of the illusion
that romantic love could be a
cure for anything.

Me   You   You

We are all the same. Made of exactly
the same stuff. Energy, light, life, whatever
you want to call it. In the sense
that there is no difference between
us, we are all one. But we are
in separate containers, and that is
an eternal truth. In that sense,
we are all alone.

"An archive of overstuffed relics...," by Alexis Roblan. Found notes on plays and dreams from before, from notebooks often crammed into backpacks and canvas bags, written on in bars and coffee shops in Manhattan and Chicago. Peeking out of the top notebook is a Los Angeles parking ticket, though the artist lives in New York City and does not own a car. In the sense that there is no difference between us, we are all one. But we are in separate containers. In that sense, we are all alone. May 14, 2020.

Everything has changed but nothing has changed.

I feel bad about how... **OK** *I feel right now.*

Like whenever someone asks:

> *Hey... How're you holding up?*

And I have to pretend an answer of-

> *Doing all right... all things considered.*

And I feel like the WORST type of person
Because I don't want to add

> *"All things considered."*

AND THERE'S A LOT OF THINGS TO CONSIDER

> *Partner lost her job*
> *Sibling diagnosed positive with Covid*
> *All my shifts at my job cancelled*
> *3 separate high profile shows postponed indefinitely*

But I'm doing OK.
I'm thriving.
I'm creating.
I'm... actually fine.

That feels weird...

> *All things considered.*

"All Things Considered," by Ashley Lauren Rogers. May 15, 2020.

← *"Beach Play," by Elaine Romero. Day before Pandemic birthday. (Photo by Bradley Wester) May 15, 2020.*

it was 5 days into quarantine when my hair started falling out
unrelated but ominous

just an equalizing of chemicals
something I'd been told to expect
but still
it was strange to see these fragments of myself
accumulating elsewhere

slithering down my back in the shower
swirling along the surface of my cup of coffee
snagging my toes as I paced and bounced and sang and paced and shushed and paced
snaking between the stack of toilet paper and the epsom salts that did nothing honestly
threading through the upholstery now speckle-stained with god knows what
hiding in the folds of his meaty little thighs

and it just kept coming and coming and coming and coming and *coming*
each shower I'd think
it has to be over right
this has to be it
there's nothing left of me to lose

but no so I let go
I poured out onto the floor
gathered in the corners
coated the baseboards

piled up in front of the doors inch by inch
climbed the walls like auburn ivy
darkened the windows until

our house
became a nest lined with me

and the chaos and the fears and the noise of today
fell away

leaving me
looking into those slate-gray eyes
stroking whisps of hair the same shade as mine

and finding

finally
a moment
of quiet

← *"postpartum," by Whitney Rowland. May 19, 2020.*

← *"Words of..." by Zoe Sarnak. May 18, 2020.*

"Self-Portrait with a Better Nose," by Matt Schatz. Doodled while on Zoomeeting. April 30, 2020.

HAMLET- ACT _____, SCENE 2
NUMBER

I have of late—but _____ I know not—lost all my
　　　　　　　　　　　ADVERB
_____, forgone all _____, and indeed it
NOUN　　　　　　　　*VERB*
goes so heavily with my _____ that this goodly
　　　　　　　　　　　　NOUN
frame, the earth, seems to me a _____ _____;
　　　　　　　　　　　　　　　ADJECTIVE　*NOUN*
this most excellent _____, the air—look you, this
　　　　　　　　　LOCATION
brave o'erhanging firmament, this majestical roof

fretted with _____ _____. Why, it appears no other
　　　　　　ADJECTIVE NOUN
thing to me than a _____ and pestilent _____ of
　　　　　　　　　ADJECTIVE　　　　　　*BODY PART*
vapors. What a piece of work is _____! How noble in
　　　　　　　　　　　　　　　　NOUN
reason, how infinite in faculty! In form and _____
　　　　　　　　　　　　　　　　　　　　　VERB
how _____ and admirable! In action how like an
　　ADJECTIVE
_____, in apprehension how like a _____! The beauty
CELEBRITY　　　　　　　　　　*MYTH*
of the world. The paragon of _____. And yet, to
　　　　　　　　　　　　　　NOUNS
me, what is this _____ of _____? Man delights
　　　　　　　　VERB　　*NOUN*
not me. No, nor _____ neither, though by your
　　　　NICE WORD FOR FEMALE
_____ you seem to say so.
ING- VERB

"Literally MAD," by Dana Schwartz. People adding their own words to make a new reality can be Wonderful or Horrible, depending on the person. And the word. May 5, 2020.

DURING THE GREAT DEPRESSION

the stately stone lions standing guard in front of New York Public Library on 42nd Street were re-christened Patience and Fortitude. Previously, they had been named after the library's astronomically wealthy donors,

which apparently didn't feel quite right in the midst of so much despair. I love those lions. Wrote in that library for years and, when my writing day was done, I'd flash them victory signs as I scaled my way down the steps. Bought a miniature version of the lions formerly known Lady Astor and Lord Lenox that I keep on my bookshelf. Or rather tried to keep. Patience slipped out of my hand a few days ago. All I am left with is Fortitude.

As a person of color, it's hard not to feel that the world always has the potential to turn terrifying on a dime. You know what happened to the ones who came before you – the trauma of the people who made the people who made you - affects you in a thousand ways you yourself will never be able to explain.

Yet, those ancestors dared to survive. Looked upon each next generation with hope and whispered, "Flourish! Flourish! Flourish!" in our ears. In my case, that meant "Go Forth and Make Theatre!" In my home, Patience got busted, but I still have Fortitude. For now, it's all I have and probably all anyone needs. The remembrances of what you and your people endured makes up not only who you are, but is a roadmap to lead you to who you must continue to aspire to be, no matter what life throws your way. What are the monuments of our own time that need new names?

← *"Save The Right Lion," by Betty Shamieh. May 12, 2020.*

SONG: **THE MAN I USED TO BE**

                          BAND
*And now, direct from the coasts of Labrador to retrieve your every
wish and whisper -- Finch & Mule singing, "The Man I Used to Be!"*

                          FINCH
I shan't elope with man nor beast, for I still hope to join the feast
and go a'crocodiling 'cross the bitter Nile.
My plan's to swing from vines instead of shooting valentines --
advancing, solipsistic, mile by mile.

A lover's arms would drag me down. I'd sooner scale the Rocky Mountains
empty-handed, save my fountain pen and steely wits.
I'll speak the secret tongue of hobos. Sail alone, hepped up on NoDoze.
Dive for El Dorado's gold where deep Atlantis sits.

                          MULE
All well and good, my friend, but meager dreams will be your end.
Why set your sites on lowly, lonely solitude?
My plans entail a throne of plenty. Me an' mine will ne'er relent,
we'll populate - through copulation, I'm renewed!

My stableful of mares comprise a har'em beyond compare --
I have the horsepow'r, to drive that rig all night.
The serfs who serve my kingdom-farm revere my name, wish Mule no harm.
My poultry, swine and chattel smile bright.

                          BOTH
And who, besides we two, could nigh accomplish what we do?
Name one who's done and lived life as have we.
M: Old Homer's guy, Odysseus.   F: That sissy's hardly worth the fuss.
F: Alexander the Great.   M: I hear he's a lousy date.
M: Lawrence of Arabia?   F: A two-faced, whiney baby - nah!
We stand alone! Just wait and see, we'll be extolled by history
in tributes to The Man I Used to Be."

                          FINCH
I've resurrected with the Incas, concocted chocolate drinks as
frothy as the nightlife in Teotihuacan.
  Shark wrestling in the Ganges with old Vishnu close at hand
That guy is "handy" in a fight, and loves to tie one on.

When I am summiting K2 (I don't use sherpas -- how 'bout you?),
the world beneath my feet, alone, I hit my stride.
"If not now, when?" were Hillel's words, so I take wing and join the birds,
and teach the Dalai Lama to relinquish pride.

                          MULE
I've never needed Bikram, get sweaty rightly quick when I'm
lounging with the lionesses in my den.
My pride is filled with wonder when they watch me spread asunder
the jaws of Jungle's King, and put my head within.

There was this bar in Guad'lahara where my chum, the russian czar,
apprised the owner that my muzzle's fire-proof.
I chewed so many habaneros, they compared me to the pharaohs --
now my gold-and-jewel'd statue crowns that roof.

                          BOTH
And who, besides we two, could nigh accomplish what we do?
Name one who's done and lived life as have we.
F: Sir Isaac Newton had gravitas.
                     M: A high-falootin' bag of gas.
M: Thomas Alva Edison?
              F: He stole from Tesla, and they were friends.
F: Pasteur, Curie, Steph'n Hawking -- Freud!
                          M: Pointy-heads leave me annoyed.
M: What about Carlton Fisk?
              F: *Yah... he was pretty good, actually.*
F: On Jeopardy Watson scored with ease.
                     M: "Dumb robots for 200, please."
M: Marc Antony envied Genghis Khan.
                     F: Richie Cunningham adored The Fonz.
M: What think ye' of the Founding Fathers?

- 273 -

"The Man I Used to Be," by Mike Shapiro. Song for a Covid-cure medicine show. May 2020. Party on.

← *"Admit One," by Jen Silverman. On the eve of the (possible) (inexorable) (ongoing) death of the American Theatre. May 9th, 2020.*

four people (or three) sit on the 'L.'

1

The first time I rode the L, my friend who was showing me the city got stuck in the door as it was closing and this guy had to help us pry the door open again so that she could get all the way into the car.

2

One time, I got on the train and there was blood on the floor next to a half-empty bottle of orange juice, and I was like, damn, somebody needed their vitamin C.

One time, I took my underwear off on the train without anybody noticing. That might sound sorta sexy, but it wasn't, it's because my underwear was too old and saggy to keep wearing.

I got on the L and this guy was staring at me all creepy, and he said, "How you doin'?" And I said, "I'm sad," and I started crying, and he went away.

I cry on the train kind of a lot.

6

I was on the train when she told me she was getting married.

When she told me

When I realized I

This train knows

Things you would

I look out the window

12

I look out the window, and I can see the lights.

- 277 -

← *"i write poems now because poems don't need a house," by Jessy Lauren Smith. May 12, 2020, or April 17-19, 2020, or sometime before.*

What is your best recipe for the future?
Would you share it?
Would you invite others to share theirs?

The future has an ancient heart. - Primo Levi

"This machine beats time: #rewritethefuture," by Elizabeth Spreen. A portal/recipe for collaboration with an unknown audience. Please send responses to e@spreen.com. May 12, 2020.

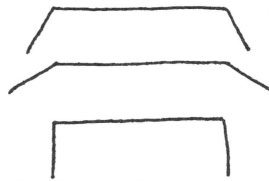

my 23rd viewing of the friends of eddie coyle

im watching a serious gangster movie from 1973
all the actors have moustaches
or acne scars
charismatic psychos
or blank toughs

the names in the credits are as follows.
Donny Van Veen
Peter Boyle
Rod Shit
Marky Mark
Ronnie Mitchum
Gilles Deleuze
Felix Guattari
Josef Albers
Simone Simons
Johnny Coma
Ricky Rachmaninoff
Josephine Silence

tenth grade lasted a decade
like sawdust on hallway vomit
and
pride in new england syntax

im watching an alligator
on the steps of the theater
eat the carcass of a medium-sized animal

the clones panic in the middle of the afternoon

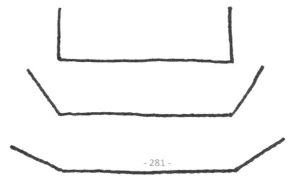

"my 23rd viewing of the friends of eddie coyle," by Matt Stadelmann. May 15, 2020.

← *"404 file not found," by Ellen Steves. May 13, 2020.*

Shallow breaths in the dark hall of desire

Grace beats its fists against fragile harbors

You and I nestled in silent prayer

Wondering how to go on

        "World goes on,"

A disembodied someone says from behind their veil of arrogance

        We clock the sounds

-World Goes

    On

Shallow tremble between us

Cos we've been through this before In the ages of silver and the ages of bronze

our distemper gets the better of us for a moment and then

okay

-    Go on, world

Break it all down

← *"Cry/sleep again," by Caridad Svich. May 10, 2020.*

I had the craziest dream last night. I woke up terrified. I never have nightmares and this one was like a high concept horror film. Like the Quiet Place which I haven't seen.

There was muffled screaming coming from this pink whirly vortex in the wall. It was awful and it wouldn't stop and when I mentioned it, she said, "You can hear that? You shouldn't be able to hear that." There was something monstrous beyond. But like literal monsters. And the child and her mother belonged in that other world and they knew what was there but weren't saying. And they slipped back and forth like it was normal.

It was terrible suffering that didn't end and it was right through the other side of the wall into whatever world was past this one.

And now I'm awake and the sun is streaming in and there are flowers everywhere and it's peaceful and the birds and the squirrels and chipmunks come for the birdseed.

I'm probably feeling guilty about being safe in my relative luxury. And I'm angry all the time. And hopeless and distraught. And this is what counts for art.

"This Is What Counts For Art," by Adam Szymkowicz. Lake Hayward, CT. May 8, 2020.

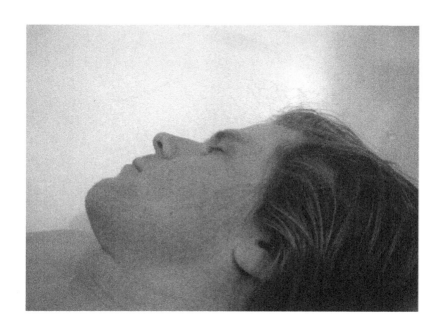

"My brain is a grand piano falling down the stairs but I'm trying to catch it," by Kate Tarker. Financial panic while watching my husband sleep. May 15, 2020.

We play cards, we play battleship, we play connect four and we connect, we connect with old friends, we disconnect, we social distance, we facetime, we skype, we g-chat, we zoom, we meet, we take meetings, we make meetings, we schedule meetings, we schedule, we plan, we break plans, we wait as plans get canceled, gigs, paychecks, weddings, appointments, vacations, months--canceled we watch shows, we watch movies, whole seasons, a whole series, we binge, we snack, we find new recipes, we make them, another meal, we think about working out . . . and we stay in and we go out (but we come right back) and we get nervous and we wash our hands and we wash our hands and we wear a face mask and we wear pajamas and we wear sweatpants and we call someone and they don't pick up, but usually they do, and we email and we computer, and we online, and we social media and we happy hour and we make a cocktail--or we do everything in our power to avoid making a cocktail or having a cigarette or doing that thing that we know we should not be doing--or maybe we are trying to do that thing that we know we should be doing, and we miss our people and we miss the gym, jesus, do we actually miss the gym? And we read a book, two, three, an article, ten, twelve, and we marvel at all the articles that we "must read," and we wonder and we feel and we feel and we feel and we start a new project and we put an old one down, we get inspired, we give up hope, we cheer out the window because it's 7pm in New York City and we hear you cheering out the window and we realize there is not just a we there is also a WE. And we wait for news and we wait to get sick. And we wait. And the world ends but it still goes on. And on. And another day. And another and another. And we go to bed. And we wake up. And we still remember and we still dream. And the sun goes to bed and the sun wakes up. And here we are. And we are alive. And we play cards...
(repeat play as many times as is necessary)

"Untitled" OR "We play cards" OR "repeat play" OR "we & WE," by Ashley Teague. Pandemic. May 12, 2020.

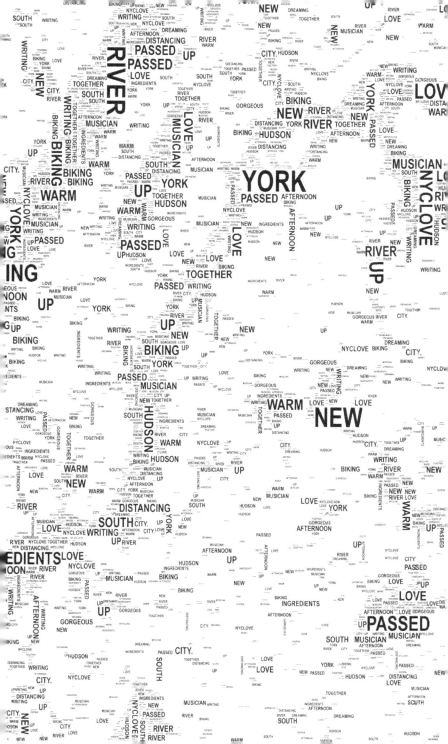

"I've Been Pandemicking Here in New York City," by Melisa Tien. A map of what being in NYC has felt like to me of late. May 17, 2020.

Virtual Meeting. Three participants look at each other. All muted. Gallery View. One person nods. Time to begin. In the chat, the following things are typed:

Person #1: I Instagrammed a photo of food I made. It wasn't even that delicious but I wanted the likes. Here's the photo:

A few moment pass.

Person #2: I alphabetized CDs I had in a box shoved way in the back of my hall closet. I will never listen to these CDs. I don't even have a CD player. I own 127 CDs.

A few moment pass.

Person #3: I was supposed to FaceTime with my parents. But I was watching porn and didn't want to stop. What's weirder is I achieved orgasm during a scene when someone just hugged someone else. It seemed so intimate.

A few moment pass. Each person leaves the meeting, not having spoken a word. End.

"Zoom Confessions," by Ken Urban. A short play for three performers in a virtual meeting. May 13, 2020.

Yup, yup, yup…

"Getting to 10,000 steps in Albany," by Kathryn Walat. An empty Empire State Plaza after bedtime. April 24, 2020.

Act One:

Act Two:

End of Play.

"I'm Still Game," by John Walch. Made during a rainstorm while thinking about anagrams. Created May 15, 2020.

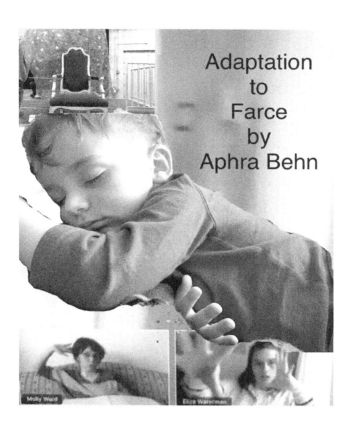

"The Permanent Womb," by Molly Ward. Loosely based on her directorial debut with Bryn Mawr College Students of her adaptation of Emperor of the Moon. OR "Now That I'm Not Directing Anymore I Have Time to Keep Nursing My Toddler," from the ongoing struggle with creation's hierarchy of values. OR "The First Play I Never Directed," from the mental din of a twenty year backlog of ideas yearning for expression. Spring 2020.

Three inner VOICES move through time and space however they damn well please.

VOICE 1

A terrible time to learn I can't draw.

There is an imperceptible shift. **Is this becoming too cinematic?** No, it lacks the gravitas for that. **Ok, thanks for the confirmation.** You're welcome.

VOICE 2

Mandatory group therapy with my inner demons.

Yes! Demons = conflict! **The self-discovery of not being able to draw didn't count?** No one cares about that. **Who made you the critic?** I did. **Well I say that a demon does not have to equal conflict.** You're right. I was profiling the demons. They might be normal and boring and inherently lacking of drama. **Isn't that what we're hoping for?** No! I want conflict! **This isn't art, this is real life. Can we agree to check the conflict at the door for the time being?** Fine... but, no one takes you seriously. **SHUT UP!**

VOICE 3

My inner demons want to know when your inner demons can come out and play.

Were you two paying any attention at all to my performance!? ... It's not all about you.

← *"The Definition of Isolation," by Seanan Palmero Waugh. Appreciation of the entertainment of the same old fears, and a preference of these over new ones. May 10, 2020.*

"The Ride," by Tatiana Wechsler. On the crest of a wave on an ordinary Thursday in Washington Heights amidst a global pandemic. May 14, 2020.

hi! hi! hi!
…hey.
HEY!
but
but what about –
NO!!!!!!!!!!!!!!!!!!!!
COME BACK!!!!!!
PLLLLEEEAAASSEEEEEEEEEEEE
NOOOOOOOOOOOOOOOOOOOOOO
WHY WOULD YOU GO IN THERE
WHILE I'M IN HERE!?!?!?!!?!?!?!?
Oh.
Hmm.
HA
Ok.
u wanna play like that?
FINE. BITCH.

i will take your blanket
and rip it up
i will take your cord
and wrap it around my neck
i will sink my teeth so deep into
this
pig
it will scream
i will roar and i will yell and i will yip
and then you'll have to come back
b/c we have neighbors & god forbid u inconvenience anybody or make
a scene I know u now I know alllllllll about u

                        and also…I <3 u
                          do u <3 me?

…   …

hi! hi! hi!
…HEY!

← *"When U Leave," by Jenny Rachel Weiner. Every time I leave the room, my puppy briefly goes insane. May 12, 2020.*

written while listening to "Faith" / George Michael / on repeat.

LOVE (AND THE APOCALYPSE) by Calamity West – 02.25.20

④ The moving of locations didn't change the desperation I was feeling when attempting to write a play about the apocalypse.

⑦ THIS PLAY WILL NEVER ~~HAPPEN~~

⑥ The map and concept of this play has died on the altar.

⑧ And I can't even bring myself to grieve the loss.

[LOVE (AND THE APOCALYPSE) by Calamity West working draft: 02.25.20]

① This is the play I started before my city went on lockdown.
   → or someone like her

⑪ And she is my favorite character.

③ Three weeks later I moved my office into the living room.

⑤ (an "Apocalypse" without the ponies.)
   ↓
   sex

⑩ All I can write about is myself.

© Calamity West – 2020

⑨ All I can stomach right now is writing comedies will watching "The Sopranos."

② Two weeks into the lockdown I turned my bedroom into an office.

← *"an apocalypse without the ponies," by Calamity West. Chicago. May 12, 2020.*

PLEASE HOLD MY HAND.

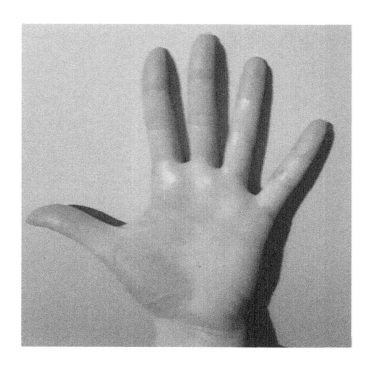

Thank you.

"Participatory theatre right now..." by Deborah Yarchun. Created in a cabin in the woods. May 9, 2020.

You come upon a Hollywood bungalow at nightfall. The air is still, mysterious, and theatre-y.
For this… is "TOUCH NO MORE": a sexy, spooky, immersive play where no one comes within six feet of each other. And all must wear masks. Cuz it's mysterious. But also, the law!

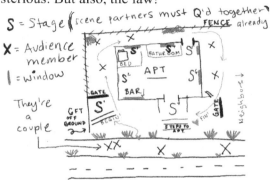

You're guided around the perimeter of the house as witches, ghosts and kings act at you, safely, through windows. You're enticed by scenes such as:

A couple writhes on a bed. There's probably fake blood and definitely kissing. But not near you! – Or, from the bathroom window, a woman washing her hands to no avail! *Wash-Wash-Covid-Metaphor!* – Or, a monologue about seeing a dagger before you. The dagger will be played by a puppet. This will make you think… *"Do I really have free will? Or am I a puppet to the whims of the powerful people around me?"* And/or, *"Should I get into puppetry?"*
Once back at the beginning, you've been left shook to your core. A leather-clad 20 something tells you never to spill the secrets of what you've seen here tonight… and also where to find them on Venmo.

"Touch No More: An Immersive Quarantine Play," by Mackenzie Yeager. She actually started writing this and drew above diagram in all seriousness months ago when she still had some form of drive in her life. March 20, 2020.

assignment for your next zoom call:

paint your thumbnail a dark color
like brown or purple or sparkly gray

plant your thumb between two of your fingers,
keeping your fingers straight
put it all up close to your laptop's camera
so that it looks like a vagina
or other genitalia of your choosing
(genitalia is vestigial now)

wiggle it around

have fun

this is theater now
you are theater

← *"i swear, if one more arts institution asks us to process the thing while we're living through the thing," by Gina Young. On feeling pressured either to monetize my response to trauma or to find a new line of work. May 7, 2020.*

the end.

-ACKNOWLEDGEMENTS-

The book-makers would like to thank the following humans:

Jordan Harrison and Adam Greenfield for their sagacity and folksy wisdom; Annah Feinberg for her steady assurance and flawless taste; the members of the Kilroys, both founding and current, for their supreme and bottomless badassery; Maria Striar for her ferociousness and her generosity; the artists in this book for being brave enough to make something and trust us with it; and **_you_**, dear reader, for purchasing this volume.

Also. To all the cherished theaters who gave us their spaces, their resources, their audiences, and their camaraderie before the pandemic… we love you. We miss you. We will see you again soon.

tripwireharlot.com

Made in the USA
Monee, IL
05 November 2020